SUCCESS WITH
THE SCROLLSAW

SUCCESS WITH THE SCROLLSAW

Zachary Taylor

The Crowood Press

First published in 1997 by
The Crowood Press Ltd
Ramsbury, Marlborough
Wiltshire SN8 2HR

British Library Cataloguing-in-Publication Data
A catalogue record for this book is available from the British Library.

ISBN 1 86126 024 5

Acknowledgements
The author thanks the following for the supply of machines and equipment for test and use in the book:
Hegner UK; Microflame Ltd (Dremel machines); Draper Tools Ltd; Rexon Ltd; J. D. Woodward Power Tools (Diamond machines); Adjustable Clamp Co.

Picture Credits
Photographs of Giovanni Aversa, Dr Aubrey Brown, Paul Budd and Stuart King were all supplied by themselves. All other photography by the author.

Line drawings produced by David Fisher.

Dedication
This book is dedicated to Derek Hooper;
good companion, good craftsman.

Typeset and designed by
D&N Publishing, Membury Business Park
Lambourn Woodlands, Berkshire.

Printed and bound by The Bath Press.

Contents

Introduction

This book is written for the woodworker, experienced or not, who uses, or is intending to use, a scrollsaw.

'Scrollsaw' is the current name for what many call the 'fretsaw', or even, 'jigsaw'. Each of the three appelations is valid, depending on one's whereabouts and in whose company one is at the time.

The scrollsaw is a prime example of a machine developed from a simple hand tool that has been used for centuries in the production of fine marquetry, intarsia and delicate pierced work. Basically, the scrollsaw imitates the action of the back-and-forth (or up-and-down) movement of hand-held saws. Its up-and-down movement, cutting only on the down-stroke (providing that the blade is fitted correctly), permits a 'both-hands hold' of the workpiece for maximum control. Maximum visibility of the saw blade, as it enters the material, is a benefit both as a safety feature and also for precise cutting.

As machines go, the scrollsaw is one of the safest to use, with few dangers, despite the speed of its action. Unlike a bandsaw or circular saw with their continuous, one-direction, blade movement, the reciprocating movement is less likely to damage careless fingers. Its nearest family member is the jigsaw, or sabresaw, which has a similar reciprocating action except that they are normally hand-held and are taken to the workpiece, rather than the other way round. If a finger accidentally touches the scrollsaw blade, just a small nick is likely to result, rather than a more serious maiming, as would almost certainly happen with its larger relatives.

Any variety of woodworking skill, from that of the raw novice to the wizard, may be accommodated by these obliging machines. Most modern examples of the scrollsaw are constructed for durability, so although their initial cost might seem relatively high, the many years of service they give and the uses to which they may be put, make sound economy. Metals and plastics may be sawn with a scrollsaw, as readily as wood, provided that the correct blades are used.

Scrollsaws are not restricted to the creation of ornamental decoration, but may also be useful for cutting small pieces around the workshop or the home, in some cases performing tasks that are impossible with other types of machine saw. Ideally suited to cutting curves from materials as thin as veneer, some machines can accommodate wood thick enough for table tops. They are also great assets in colleges and schools as teaching aids and for general sawing.

One of the more attractive features of the scrollsaw to the home craftsman is its portability, enabling the worksite to be moved from room to room if need be. Some models, of course, are not mobile, being intended for heavier, production work and these are usually mounted on a substantial free-standing support rather than on a bench.

A wide choice of machines is available currently, each with its own features to attract craftworkers in different ways, depending on their needs. Whichever variety is owned, a thorough knowledge of its operation and maintenance will enable the owner to get the best from it.

Apart from describing the basic function of the scrollsaw, this book provides many examples of its uses, together with advice from the author, who has been one of the tool's most enthusiastic exponents for many years, incorporating it into his professional life as a luthier, journalist and tutor.

1 The History and Development of the Scrollsaw

Early on in man's use of blades there must have occurred the discovery that a serrated edge was more efficient at cutting than a plain sharp edge. Certain bones and shells, such as jaw-bones and scallop shells, have a natural serration that possibly led to the inspiration for the saw.

Thinner blades mean less waste and less effort needed in the sawing operation, but thinner blades also mean less control, unless they are supported at either end. Possibly the archery bow gave ideas for the design of the frame that is now commonly used to hold the blade and keep it in tension.

Sizes of blades and their complementary frames ranged widely, as they still do, and although the earliest tools no longer exist, the work by the ancient sawyers does, serving as silent witness to the skills of the past. Examples of decorative inlay, dated as early as 3,000 BC, suggest that fine blades were used to shape patterns and forms very early in the application of encrustation.

A hand-powered scrollsaw, or fretsaw, in company with its larger relatives, the coping saw, hacksaw and bowsaw, featured a means of attaching the ends of the blade to the ends of the C-frame.

Spring in the metal frame kept the blade taut. In repose, the metal frame was wider across its opening than the blade, thus

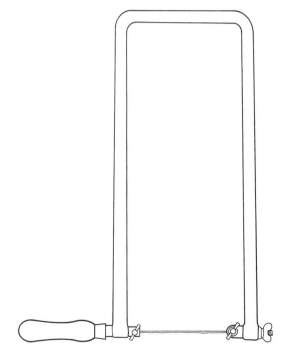

Fig. 1 Common fretsaw frame for manual use. Its simplicity belies the accuracy with which a skilled person can operate it. Some of the finest examples of scrollsawing are still produced this way, but professionals now generally use machine scrollsaws.

8

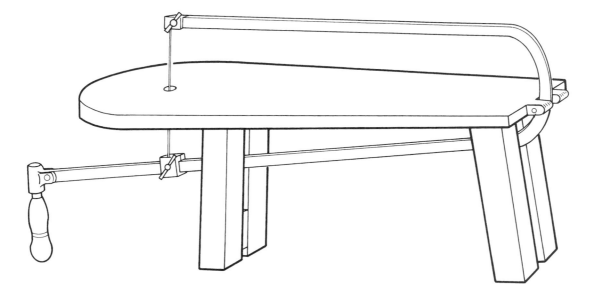

Fig. 2 A simple mechanized, manually operated, C-frame scrollsaw.

necessitating its closure under compressive pressure whilst the blade was attached. In 'closing-up' the ends of the C-frame, the blade itself provided the stability required of the tool.

Usually, a handle was incorporated at the end of one of the frame's arms, in line with the blade.

The transition from manual to mechanical application appears to have begun in the nineteenth century with the invention of the 'donkey', possibly taking its name from the fact that it had supporting legs and was sat upon to operate it. Its two main features were the attachment of the frame in a slide that was activated manually in a horizontal, push-pull, motion and a foot-operated clamp to retain the workpiece. This design uses a rigid frame made essentially from wood and maintains the blade in constant tension, unlike its cousin with a spring return.

The latter, examples of which still exist abundantly in European museums, has a vertical blade operation. Its frame, largely made from wooden members, has a bow- or cart-spring attached horizontally to its top member, suspended over a table. One end of a saw blade is clamped into the upper jaw connected to the spring, its other end is passed through a hole in the table and is clamped to a lower jaw. A treadle is attached to the lower jaw, permitting downward movement of the blade by pressing with the foot. During this action, the spring becomes partially deformed by tension transmitted through the blade; when pressure is released, the spring recovers its form and draws back the blade to its original position. Repetition produces the characteristic reciprocating action of the scrollsaw.

Treadling as a means of providing power was effective but tiring and one can readily

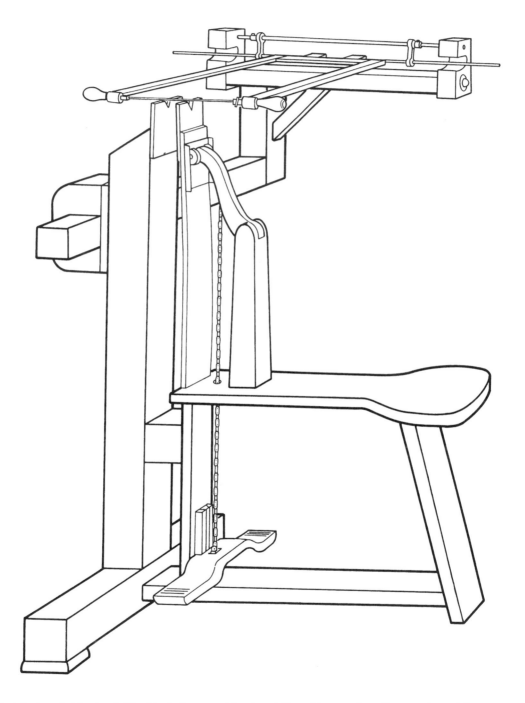

Fig. 3 A fretwork 'donkey'. The blade is moved horizontally with a push-pull operation of the right hand, leaving the left hand to manipulate the workpiece. Intended for operation whilst sitting, with the foot-operated work-holder conveniently sited for both feet.

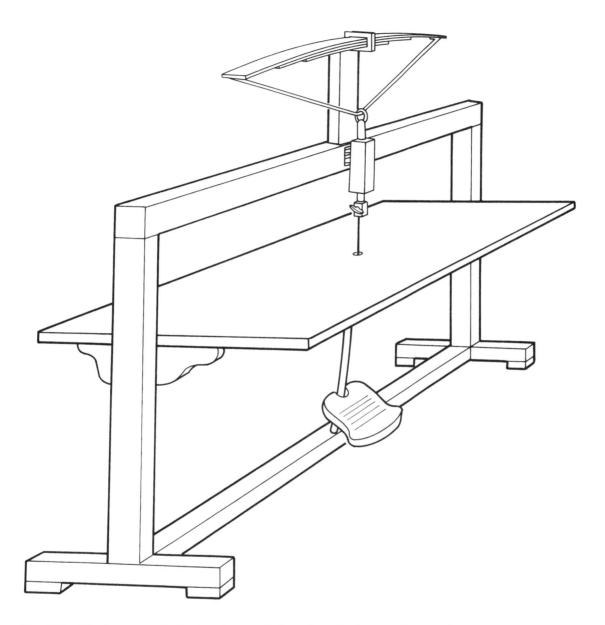

Fig. 4 Used for large panels, the treadle-operated scrollsaw had an overhead spring-return.

see how the pedal mechanism, after the style of the bicycle, had greater appeal. Converting the rotary action to produce a reciprocating, up-and-down, movement, was a stepping stone to the versions of today powered by electric motor.

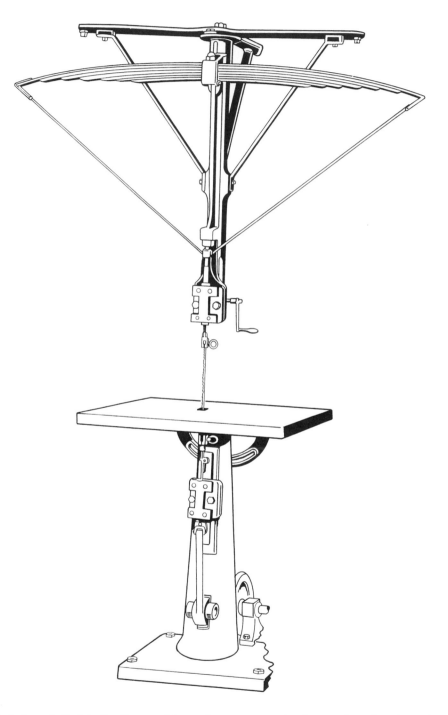

Fig. 5 With its base bolted to the floor and its spring-return mechanism anchored to the ceiling, this scrollsaw has no chance of escape! It is an early motorized version, built to last and to cut maximum depths with great precision.

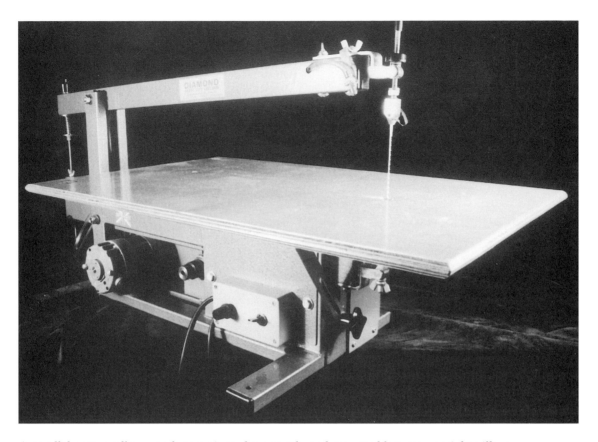

A parallel-arm scrollsaw, each arm pivoted separately and mounted between upright pillars.

Both the rigid frame and the spring-return types have been modified to accept motorization; they form the bedrock of all subsequent scrollsaw development.

Spring-return types are becoming less common, giving way generally to the parallel-arm and C-frame variety. These will be examined closely later, but in mechanical function they have little in common, as this brief description shows.

The parallel-arm type has both upper and lower arms fitted horizontally on pivots, to a rigid vertical column. When the blade is fixed between the two arm-ends it makes the fourth side of a parallel-ogram. It follows that the arms move simultaneously and equally, resulting in a vertical movement of the saw blade.

The C-frame is shaped like an elongated letter 'C', at whose open ends the saw-blade is attached. The single pivot permits the frame to swing vertically through a radius, and therefore the blade cannot be moving truly vertically. The distance of the pivot from the blade and its vertical position in relation to the table both have a part to play in determining the motion of the blade and how closely the arc described by the blade approximates to a vertical motion.

A typical C-frame scrollsaw. Its rear part is enclosed by the casing, but its pivot can be seen protruding from the side-wall above the back leg.

Each type of machine has its strengths and weaknesses, its virtues and faults. Often as not, critics of one type will be discounted by its successful exponents. Within few limits, the range of work producible by one machine may be produced on them all, leaving the final choice to the individual. It is a wide choice...

2 Machine Types and Features

Scrollsaws come in a variety of shapes and sizes, although for ease of classification we may group them by their mechanical action thus:
1. parallel-arm
2. C-frame
3. spring return.
Machines may be portable or static, though in most cases, with the exception of the heavier industrial types, static scrollsaws are simply portable ones bolted to stands often designed and supplied by the manufacturer. It is in the nature of the scrollsaw to have a tendency to vibrate and therefore it is advisable, in the case of the handy lightweight types, to clamp or bolt them onto a bench or table for stability.

Six of the best! A small selection of the many scrollsaws currently available. Left is a C-frame type, the rest are all parallel-arm machines.

Let us now look at the three basic types separately

1. Parallel-arm Type

These have upper and lower arms operating in parallel, pivoted independently but in line, on a vertical column. A parallelogram is achieved by the fixing of the blade between the two arm-ends, thus acting as its fourth side. The photograph illustrates the principle.

Since the upper and lower arms are pivoted on the column, with pivots on the blade fixings at each end of the arms, it follows that any vertical movement of one arm is reciprocated by the other. One of the features of this type of action is that, once set correctly, the blade remains vertical to the table-plane. This is claimed as a paramount requirement by the suppliers of this type of machine.

Parallel-arm machines generally use a blade-tensioning system that requires the adjustment of the rear arm-connection. Usually this is in the form of a threaded rod attached at each end to the ends of the arms and fitted with a nut, or a knob of some sort, to adjust the tension by reducing or increasing the distance between the arms.

In most cases, the parallel-arm types have a limited adjustment to accommodate the common, nominally-sized, 127mm (5in) blade length. Many users enjoy this limited but reliable feature,

Both arms are exposed in this machine, showing the pivoting and the parallel action.

preferring not to have to make adjustments to the basic geometry of the machine. A few machines have an extendable opening of the arms, allowing the use of a wide range of blade lengths and types, increasing the versatility of the machine enormously.

Often, the parallel-arm machine will have a cover enclosing the arms, effectively hiding the movement from view. This may be seen as a safety feature, in that there is almost no contact possible with the moving upper arm. However, other people may see this as a handicap, if access is needed to the mechanism, particularly in the case of the lower arm, during blade changing. Some machines are extremely inconvenient in this respect.

2. C-frame Type

The C-frame is shaped like a one-piece elongated letter 'C', at whose open ends the saw-blade is attached. At the closed, opposite end, there is a pivot permitting movement of the frame. Clearly, as the movement is a limited part of a radius, it must therefore follow that the blade cannot be moving truly vertically. Many claim this lack of verticality to be inferior to the action of a parallel arm type. Others, however, feel that the up-stroke, effectively withdrawing the teeth of the blade from the cut face, is an advantage, in that less pressure is applied on the withdrawal. One might assume that if a sawblade is not reciprocating vertically, it must inevitably

Compact design and portability are benefits of this small C-frame machine. Note the dust-extraction port at the front of the machine below the saw-table.

hamper the movements necessary for tight curves. (See 'Theory, geometry and practice', below.)

An advantage of the C-frame is that tensioning of the blade is usually achieved by adjusting the position of the blade-holder by means of cams, or levers, and this mechanism is sited conveniently on top of the upper arm. Many incorporate a quick-release detensioning device that helps in blade-changing.

3. Spring Return Type

A rigid upper frame incorporating a spring-loaded blade holder is the common feature of this type of machine. A lower clamp is moved vertically whilst the spring maintains tension in the blade. Downward movement extends the spring, whose contraction maintains the tension on the blade on the up-stroke. Unfortunately, the blade tension is not constant, which is detrimental to efficiency. The larger industrial machines, now somewhat dated, are gradually being set aside in favour of the parallel-arm type. Domestic craftsmen are unlikely these days to come across this variety of scrollsaw.

THEORY, GEOMETRY AND PRACTICE

Various merits or faults are set out in tests, reports, manuals and literature on the subject of the action of parallel-arm and C-frame types of scrollsaw.

Theory says that the parallel-arm reciprocates and keeps the sawblade permanently vertical, whilst the C-frame moving on a single pivot must therefore cause the reciprocating blade to describe an arc. This theory is virtually irrefutable.

Theory goes on to presume that the parallel-arm type will follow a tighter curve more efficiently due to the smaller kerf left by the saw. Protagonists of the C-frame type believe that the slight withdrawal of the blade relieves pressure on the upstroke, and thus creates less wear on the teeth. Parallel-arms, on the other hand, are said to produce a better finish on the sawn sides of the kerf because of the 'cleaning' of the cut by the blade during the upstroke.

Looking at the geometry of the two types of action, to help in the assessment of their merits or faults, linked with the foregoing propositions, one may consider the following. Parallel arms, provided they are correctly set, will move the sawblade vertically in both up- and down-strokes. Unfortunately, most of this type have no adjustment fore and aft, so this function is dependent on the accuracy of the manufacturer's production procedures. Happily, these are generally adequate.

For comparison, let us examine the geometry of the action of a C-frame saw.

Take, as a nominal example, a machine with a 500mm (20in) throat and a 25mm (1in) stroke fitted with a 125mm (5in) blade. If the bearing were located at point 'B', then at the up-stroke, point 'A' would have risen by 25mm (1in), or put another way, the line 'C–B' would rise by 3°

> Checking for perpendicularity of the saw blade may be achieved by placing a square block in contact with the blade at the extremity of its down-stroke. Hold the block in the same position as the arms are moved, by turning the drive manually, to the extremity of the up-stroke. The blade should be in constant contact throughout the movement if the parallel action is correctly set.

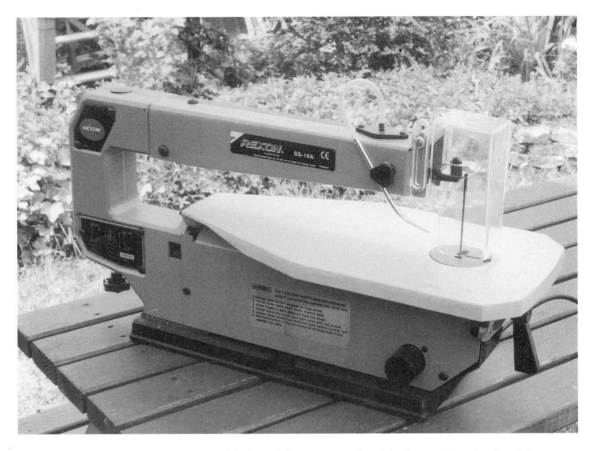

Throat depth is measured between the blade and the rear upright of the frame. Note the dust blower nozzle attached by a bracket to the upper casing. Adjustment of the latter is possible, both radially and fore-and-aft.

approximately. In this geometrical arrangement there would be a theoretical blade 'withdrawal' on the upstroke, of about 0.625mm (0.025in) at 25mm (1in) above the table. This assumes the bearing is level with the table.

In practice, there is little doubt that the parallel action produces a marginally cleaner cut face and permits the negotiation of smaller radii. These considerations are nevertheless relative to the class of work to be undertaken and the costs of the respective machines.

WHICH FEATURES?

Throat Size

Throat size will probably play a part in deciding which machine suits the work, simply because this limits the size of workpiece that may be passed between the blade and the rear frame.

Throat depth sizes vary from 350mm (13in) to about 650mm (25in), so the individual should consider the scale of work planned to help make the correct choice.

Some practical suggestions on this topic are found in Chapter 8.

Depth of Cut

This is generally around 50mm (2in) maximum, although one or two exceptions will handle more; the Diamond, for example, will accommodate a 28mm (11in) long hacksaw blade for metal cutting!

When cutting to the maximum capacity of the machine, it is necessary to use a heavy blade structure with a coarse toothing to reduce to a minimum the tendency for the blade to bow in the centre of the cut. This condition is almost inevitable, making turns difficult if other than ideal conditions are applied.

Cutting Speed

Cutting speeds are stated in terms of strokes per minute (s.p.m.). Some of the smaller machines are available with single speed only, some with a choice of two speeds, whilst others have variable speeds from zero to over a thousand s.p.m.

This latter feature may seem relatively unimportant until one considers the application of different materials. Take a spread of materials from softwoods to hard, from veneers to planks, plastics to metals, and an appreciation of the facility to change speed comes into perspective.

Fixed, one-speed machines come at around 1500 s.p.m., more or less, and are adequate for general purpose work. They will cope with a large range of material densities and thickness with correct blades and feeds (*see* Chapter 3).

Two-speed machines are now few and far between; those with variable speed controls are more common and they come with speeds ranging from as little as 700/1,600, to 0/1,600. Up to 2,000 s.p.m. is available if super-high speeds are necessary, in this case, the operator will probably be working on veneer and needs to be highly skilled!

Length of Stroke

It does not necessarily follow the theory that the thickness must be less than or equal to the stroke length, but there is no doubt that the longer the stroke, the greater the thickness of material one can cut.

Strokes vary in length from machine to machine, from less than 10mm (around ⅜in) up to 30mm (almost 1¼in), with a common length of about 19mm (say ¾in).

Few machines have stroke adjustment, but those that have permit some useful flexibility. Typically, with an adjustable stroke, one would establish from inspection of the stroke range available the relevant thicknesses of materials balanced against blade type and material density. The latter would vary according to either wood, fibre, metal, plastic or what-have-you. It is difficult to recommend firm figures because of the multitude of variables, therefore a trial and error basis must apply to get the best from the equipment. As a general rule, though, use a short stroke for veneers and metal sheet, graduating up to maximum stroke length for thicker stuff. Remember, the major concern is not so much cutting the material as removing the waste it creates.

Motor Power

Small capacity machines use correspondingly small motors, but not all larger machines follow a vice-versa rule. For instance some makes offer several machines of widely differing capacity in terms of stroke, speed and throat depth, yet using the same motor. By the nature of commercial practice, as one might expect, they will claim that the large machine is adequately powered whilst the small one has enough and some to spare. Perhaps it is true. Normal use of the scrollsaw rarely defeats the available motor power, so the average user need not feel sceptical about inadequacy in this feature.

Even so, the range is very wide, from units of less than 80 watts up to 375 watts. Larger motors, coupled with variable speed controls, must undoubtedly give less trouble over a greater period of time.

Dust Blowers

The production of sawdust from operating a scrollsaw is relatively small and may be fine enough to look like flour. The fact is, however, that over time quantities can build up to a troublesome level unless steps are taken to remove it as it is created. Clearing the dust from the work area may be simply achieved by sending jets of air directed at the point where the saw blade enters the material. This achieves the objective of clearing dust from the cutting line.

Length of stroke is determined by the mechanism converting from rotary to reciprocating motion. In this case, the connecting-rod is attached to the frame and the motor spindle with a counterbalance weight.

Motor power is usually related to the capacity of the machine. In this case, a heavy-duty affair, the motor is 375 watts. It also has an independent dust blower with its own motor.

'Dust blower' is somewhat of a misnomer, in that, most movement of air supplied for this purpose is generated by small bellows activated by the reciprocation of the frame. Thus as the frame moves downwards it compresses the bellows. The air is piped to the proximity of the saw blade, escaping in puffs. 'Dust puffer' would therefore be a more descriptive name for this device. A few makes of scrollsaw use a pump that operates independently of the mechanical action of the frame, thus giving a constant flow of compressed air. This system provides more air, under greater compression, and is more efficient.

Dust Extraction

This is done by collecting dust via the extraction port, provided one is fitted. Location of the port is the main consideration and since the majority of the dust is drawn through the workpiece down below the saw-table, this is obviously where the orifice inlet should be. In some cases, the port is incorporated into the lower machine casing projecting its outlet forward to receive a connection to a vacuum extraction device.

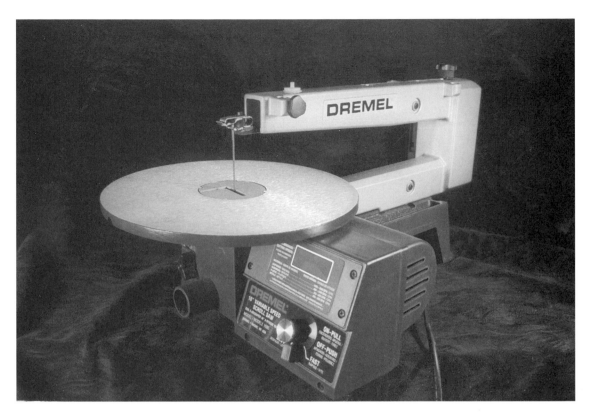

Blade-holders are a permanent fixture on this machine and they are intended for pin-end blades. Adaptors are fitted to accept plain blades if required.

Blade-holders

Blades are held in place at the ends of the top and bottom frames by clamps. Some type of screw device, operated by a key of some sort, is the most usual method of blade retention.

They vary in design, from fussy and clumsy to fast and efficient. It may matter to some that the faster means better, and providing that the clamping is secure, it is a view that I personally hold. All blade-holders have their idiosyncrasies, but with familiarity these become more acceptable.

Both pin-end and plain blades need to be catered for, and this requires either a holder that accommodates both types or one that accepts adaptors for both. Many are equipped to receive pin-end blades as standard, with adaptors to hold plain blades.

I regard pin-end blades as a quick-fit, general purpose carpentry tool, since by their physical nature they are coarse toothed and heavy in construction. In this case, a holder that requires to be adapted for plain blades is less convenient than the all-purpose variety that receives either type of blade.

Some holders need to be removed from the frames for blade loading, while others remain *in situ*, with clear advantages

23

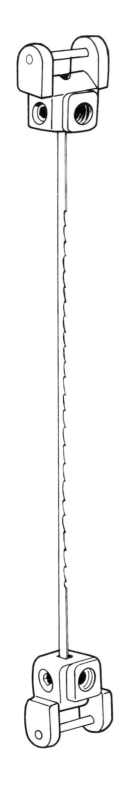

during 'threading' of blades for aperture sawing, since only the upper end of the blade need be detached.

Holders that need to be removed from the frames for blade loading reduce the efficiency of the machine for aperture cutting, since the blade-threading must take place with the blade and holder removed from the frame. If the workpiece is relatively large this may present problems of handling, particularly if the blade is very fine. Risk of blade breakage is high. Best use a machine with the facility to load blades without removal of the holders, if the majority of the work programme is aperture cutting.

Fig. 6 A plain blade held in the type of holders shown in Fig. 11. The lower arm has the same bracket as the top. Care must be taken to ensure that the blade is mounted the correct way, with teeth pointing downwards, when attaching to the machine.

3 Blades and Blade-holders

The saw edge represents, and indeed functions, as a row of small chisels, each removing a tiny portion as they are drawn across the material. It will be apparent that the design and arrangement of the teeth is of paramount importance to the performance of the blade. Spacing, pitch and angles are some of the considerations facing the manufacturer and the user, in determining the blade's design.

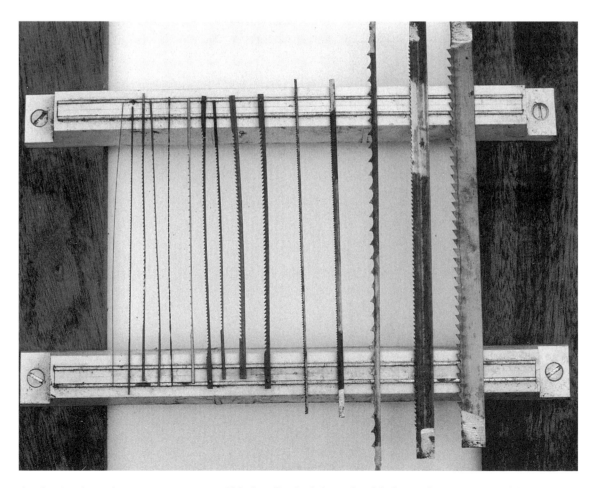

A selection from the enormous range of blades. On the left are fine blades as thin as 0.29mm (about 12 thousandths of an inch). The three largest, on the right, are converted from bandsaws and hacksaws. Machines with the facility to accept these latter are rare.

In all probability, sawyers have demanded blades to cope with their different needs and blade-makers have provided them. This kind of collaboration still pertains, I hope. Time was, when a sawyer had to make his own blades, but I prefer not to contemplate that!

Teeth

Of the various features of the blade, one of its main reference points is its number of teeth, called the 'pitch' and specified by the amount in an imperial inch – hence 12 t.p.i., for example, means 12 teeth per inch.

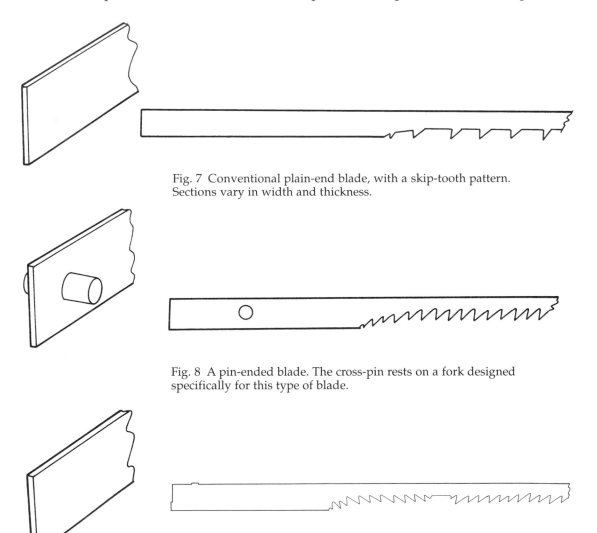

Fig. 7 Conventional plain-end blade, with a skip-tooth pattern. Sections vary in width and thickness.

Fig. 8 A pin-ended blade. The cross-pin rests on a fork designed specifically for this type of blade.

Fig. 9 Reverse toothing on a blade intended to cut on the upstroke as well as down. Usually, the lowest half-dozen teeth are arranged in this manner on such a blade.

A fine toothing will have as many as 80 t.p.i, for cutting metals, whilst the coarse end of the range has less than 10 t.p.i.

Material removed by each tooth has to find space, or jamming takes place, resulting in burning rather than cutting. Gaps between teeth provide the space for the dust or 'swarf', and depending on the amount of waste being cut by the tooth, so must the gap correspond. It is usual to have a gap at least equivalent to the length of the tooth, in some cases, double that. As a general rule, the thicker the material being cut, the bigger the gap needs to be between the teeth.

Blades for metals are made from harder steel and produced with less set on the teeth. The term 'set' refers to the amount of projection by the points of the teeth, either side of the width of the blade.

Fig. 10 For cutting a curve without rotating the workpiece; a spiral blade that cuts in any direction. It may be seen that it is made by twisting an otherwise flat blade into a spiral.

Some special variations include reverse teeth. In this design, at one end of the blade, usually about six teeth point in the opposite direction to the main row of teeth.

When loaded conventionally, with teeth pointing downwards, the lower 'reversed' teeth are therefore pointing upwards. This is said to produce a cleaner cut, leaving smoother sides to the sawn face. In practice it seems to do so, though naturally there is a greater tendency to lift the workpiece on the upstroke.

Another type of blade is twisted into a spiral, thus offering the possibility to saw in any direction, a circle for example, without changing the position of the workpiece radially. These tend to be somewhat coarse leaving a comparatively rough finish, but there may be some applications where this may not be important.

If a wide range of materials and thicknesses are used, then it follows that a corresponding range of blades will be needed. Some machines are provided with devices that can hold anything, from nail files to pieces of old hacksaw blade, with the obvious advantages to the lucky owner.

Back to the Past

In times gone by, it was possible to purchase blades that had rounded backs, rather than the sharp square corners of the current product. Rounded corners means easier negotiation of sharp turns.

Whilst it is regrettable that modern producers do not, for whatever reason, supply blades with this feature, there is a remedy. After loading the blade into the frame, set the machine moving at a slow speed if available, and bring an abrasive device into contact with the rear corners of the blade. This device may be a small sanding block fitted with emery cloth, or some

As the blade reciprocates, the abrasive stone is held against its back corners to round and smooth the surface for ease of negotiating tight curves.

other metallic abrasive, or a carborundum stone intended for sharpening chisels. Bear in mind that the operation is severely damaging to a sharpening stone, due to the localized friction from the slender blade, so best to use an old one and keep it for this purpose. The object is to smooth and round the back corners of the blade, so this must be envisaged during the manipulation of the abrader. This simple process is one of the most effective improvements accessible to all sawyers, at almost no cost.

Grading of Blades

As one might imagine, with a craft as old as fretwork and its modern day equivalent, scrollsawing, the range of blade types is enormous. Inconsistency of reference doesn't help when trying to assess one's requirements from suppliers' catalogues. Although an attempt was made to standardize by Universal Generic Number (U.G.No), not all manufacturers use this coding system. Even in this sensible-sounding idea, there are two scales: one for wood and one for metals, meaning that unless you are knowledgeable about tooth design and can spot the difference at a glance, there is little use knowing the U.G.No.

Metalworking blades do not have the 'skip-tooth' pattern normally associated with woodworking blades, so that should help identify the two types. As far as wood-working blades are concerned, U.G.Nos go from 2/0, being about 0.55mm (0.022in) wide, with a thickness of 0.25mm (0.010in) and 28t.p.i. These increase in about a dozen steps to No 12, about 1.7mm (0.067in) wide and 0.5mm (0.020in) thick with 9.5t.p.i.

The code for metalworking blades is as follows: the U.G.No 0/8 blade is approximately 0.3mm (0.012in) in width, 0.15mm (0.006in) thick with 84t.p.i. At the other end of the range is the U.G.No 12 blade, about 1.75mm (0.070in) wide, by 0.575mm (0.023in) thick with 17t.p.i.

Generally, suppliers will offer a selection of blades from within this range, designated with their own catalogue references, so it is safest to ask for details: width, thickness, t.p.i. etc. to ascertain the design before ordering in bulk. A rule of thumb is simple: the thinner the material, the thinner the blade, and vice versa. For beginners, ask for a selection; most suppliers offer a sample pack, but do find out 'which' is 'what', to facilitate reordering on a knowledgeable basis.

BLADE-HOLDERS

The problems associated with blade retention are one of the major considerations confronting the designer of the scrollsaw frame, and in this feature lies much of the tool's potential efficiency.

The type of work undertaken by the user will determine the type of blade-holder most required. Variety of work equals variety of needs. Clamps, closed by means of screws, have been the common method used to hold the blade-ends, with many variations on that simple theme. An alternative to the clamping principle is that of the 'pin-ended' blade system. This uses blades with a hole pierced at either end fitted with pins that project either side of the blade.

The pins rest in small brackets attached to the ends of the frames. Usually, these

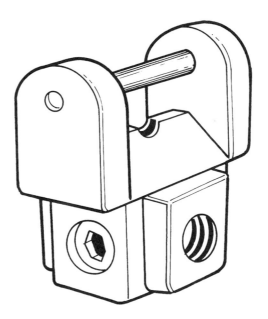

Fig. 11 This type of blade-holder grips plain-ended blades by tightening two opposing grub-screws to meet the blade in the centre of the clamp. Its 'stirrup' bar is used to attach it to the pin-ended blade holder, thus converting from one type to the other. Blades may be turned through 90 degrees by changing the position of the grub-screws to the other threaded holes.

Loading the blade is assisted here by the incorporation of recesses in the machine casing. The holders are retained in the recesses at the correct distance for the loading of a standard plain-end blade.

brackets incorporate small stirrups, to which may be attached clamping devices to hold plain blades.

Pin-ended Blades

In my case, pin-end blades are almost never used since my own use of the scroll-saw is for the relatively fine and delicate workpiece that excludes the use of the coarse and heavy-gauge blade. The holder for pin-end blades is generally uncomplicated, so little need be said about it, other than the frame-end is fitted with a bracket bearing a slot.

The blade is inserted into the slot, and as tension is applied, the pins are held by the bracket. The pins fit into small recesses and are thus firmly anchored, preventing withdrawal when the blade is subjected to forward thrust.

Plain-ended Blades

Dealing with the plain-ended blade then, is a different subject. If one is in the company

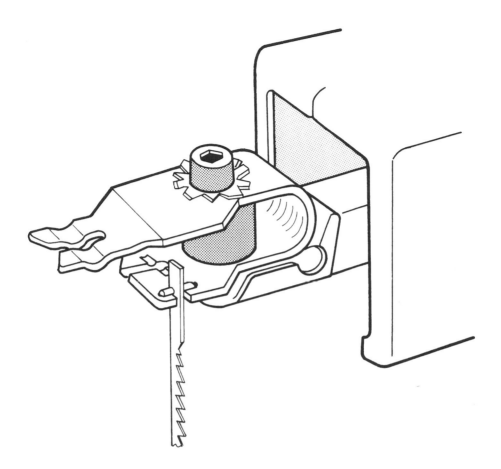

Fig. 12 An upper arm blade-holder, designed especially for pin-ended blades. It may be adapted for plain blades with the 'stirrup' holder shown in Fig. 11.

Quick-change Holders

of enthusiasts of the scrollsaw and the conversation is lagging, open up the topic of blade-holders and things brighten up. In fact, it is possible that some heat will be generated as the various merits and flaws of different types are discussed.

Up to a point, preferences are a question of familiarity – the breeder of efficiency, in my opinion, not necessarily contempt. Even so, some designs of holder lend themselves to ease of operation and others less so.

The operator who cuts a lot of apertures needs a means of fast blade changing. Convenience of clamping, combined with retention of the lower end of the blade to facilitate threading, is essential.

Of the varieties that necessitate the removal of the holders from the frame in order to load the blade, few are fast enough to attract, for example, a serious marquetarian, or anyone producing fine

31

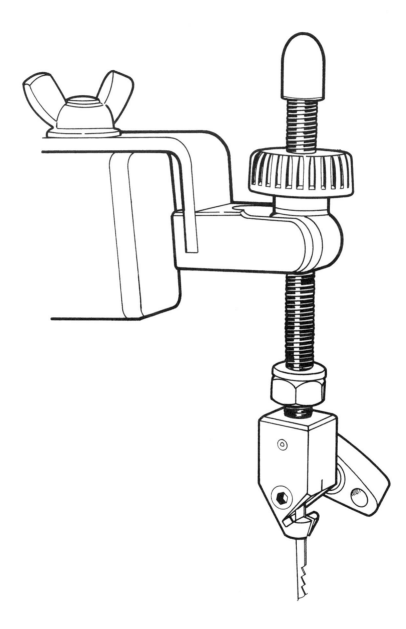

Fig. 13 Blade-holder attached to the upper arm of the Diamond scrollsaw. Note, the clamp may be used to hold either the pin-ended or plain blades. The knurled upper screw adjusts tension and the lower hexagon nut is screwed up underneath the extension to lock it. The latter is shown here in the unlocked position.

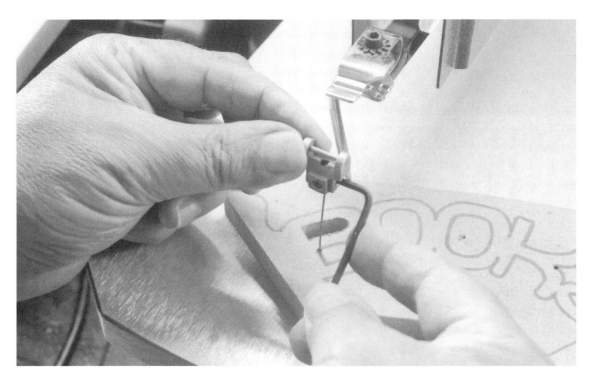

A tricky loading job where apertures are being cut, since the threading of the blade must take place before the holder is attached. The subsequent reattachment needs patience and a little time.

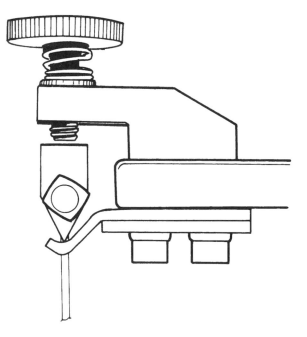

Fig. 14 The vee-shape of the clamp brings it into vertical alignment in the support when tension is applied by the upper knurled screw.

fretwork. Not to mention the difficulties experienced with the handling of large workpieces, where the dangers of blade breakage is high.

In one case at least, although the manufacturer has no fast-change holder, compensation is made by offering a means of securing the lower end of the blade whilst the upper part is released, to permit the threading of the blade through the access hole in the workpiece. News of a development to improve this even further has just been released by Hegner.

In addition to the standard holder supplied with the Diamond saw, in itself permitting a faster change than most standard holders, the manufacturer offers a quick-action version, a simple design featuring a hole in the clamping block into which the blade is inserted. Centralization is therefore immediate and automatic; retention is then a simple matter of tightening the screw knob by hand.

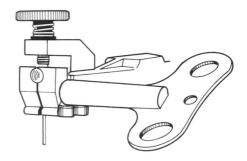

Fig. 15 A slotted clamp, tightened with a screw by means of a type of clock-key, is a Hegner feature.

Machines constructed on the C-frame principle often have a swing lever with which to apply and release blade tension. This reduces the change time by eliminating the need to turn the tensioning devices found normally on parallel-motion saws.

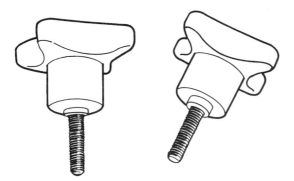

Fig. 16 Plastic knobs may be used as an alternative to the clock-key, to speed-up blade changing.

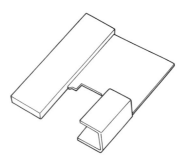

Fig. 17 Especially designed for reducing 'threading' time when cutting apertures; this jig holds the Hegner upper clamp steady when the blade is detached.

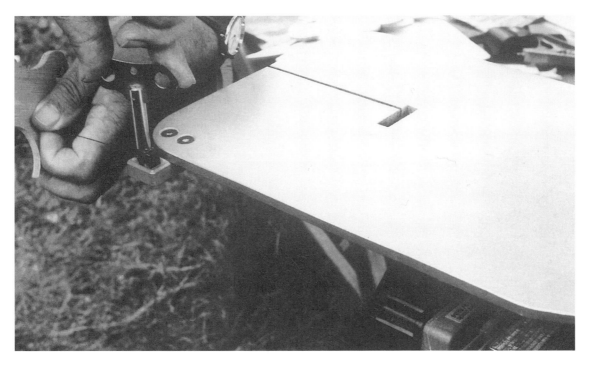

Not a particularly fast change, but a secure one in which the blade-holder is placed in a secure socket whilst the blade is inserted. Again, tricky if 'threaded' work is to be undertaken.

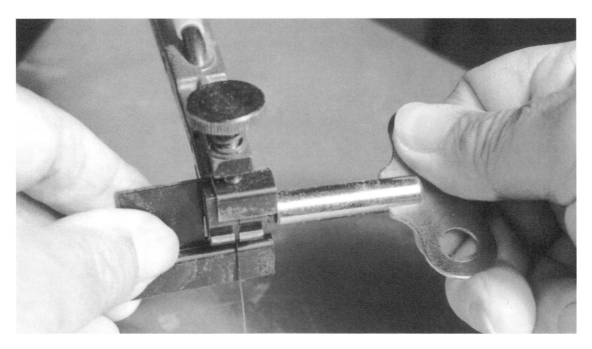

Same holder as above but with a retaining jig applied to facilitate quick change of blade for threading through work. Only the upper end of the blade is freed for this operation.

4 Accessories

Stands

If workshop space is a premium, a bench-top model may be the answer, with the possibility of storing it away during periods of machine down-time. Even so, it is advisable to fix the saw by clamping it down to the worktop surface for a 'quick-fix', or bolting for more permanent security, even for short spells. The machine, after all, uses

Saws should be clamped to a bench or, as in this case, to a stand. Whether dedicated to its own saw, or home-made for the purpose, a stand makes sense, provided that there is space for it in the workshop.

A suggestion if bolting down, whether on a bench or stand: use a rubber compound or some similar material to make washers for insertion between the machine and the stand surface, to reduce the transmission of vibration and sound. A recycled carpet tile is ideal for this job, although some proprietary brands of insulation materials are available for the fastidious operator.

a reciprocating action and this combined with horizontal pressure from the work-pieces creates a tendency for it to move during sawing.

Some manufacturers supply stands as optional extras that effectively transform a mobile saw into a static one, inasmuch as the machine may stay put permanently in one spot if desired. Even so, the stand-mounted saw may be moved if need be, since the assembly rarely exceeds a weight sufficient to preclude movement. Some owners may feel inclined to bolt down the stand to the workshop floor for extra stability, and few would argue with the principle.

Whether the purpose-designed stand or a home-spun variety is used matters little, as long as the machine is immobilized. An advantage of a self-made stand is that it may be custom built to the user's needs, working-height and so on.

Whether the operator shall stand or sit depends on the kind of work to be under-taken; if used infrequently on small pieces, then like as not a standing pose is conve-nient. If, on the other hand, the saw will be employed often and for long periods, some merit lies in the operator being seated. A seated pose is not only less tiring but one's concentration is given to sawing without the concern for balance, and such things as the operation of a foot-switch are more easily controlled. (More about footswitches below.)

Stands supplied by manufacturers are normally metal structures made from fab-ricated frames or folded sheet metal. Self-made stands may be made from metal or wood, and provided that a work bench is available initially, the scrollsaw may be used to make a custom stand, by the oper-ator for themselves. A stand that incorpo-rates storage not only keeps the machine's accessories conveniently to hand but also adds beneficial weight to the structure. See the illustrations of custom stands for some basic ideas.

Footswitches

Part of the security of the sawing opera-tion and the control of the moving work-piece is through the sensitive contact of the hands. There is little need to say any more than this to qualify the need to attach a footswitch for the connection and discon-nection of electricity to the scrollsaw.

A footswitch should be regarded as one of the most essential features of a scroll-saw, and not simply a desirable 'extra'. The frequency with which the work needs to be halted during the sawing operation may be high, depending on its type. In this case, the facility to stop and restart the sawing without the need to remove the hands is most useful.

Even more advantageous is the foot-switch that controls speed of operation as well as power supply. Not an essential per-haps, but anyone who has used one will tell you that it is well worth considering as an adjunct for precision work, allowing such facilities as slow starts followed by gradual increase of speed, then slowing down to negotiate tricky portions. Again, an objective appraisal of the type of work to be undertaken is essential at the plan-ning stage of life with a scrollsaw.

Some thoughtful manufacturers offer footswitches as an option; if not, then it is relatively easy for the owner of the machine to acquire and fit one. Its positioning is critical and must be carefully considered. Two major factors are involved, that of its location to be convenient to the foot while, at the same time, keeping it out of the way of accidental operation.

When a footswitch is fitted, it is likely to work best if it is attached to a footrest raised up from the floor, thus answering the need to rest the foot and prevent unintended activation of the switch.

Fences

Sawing straight lines is harder to achieve on scrollsaws than, say, a bandsaw, because the relatively thin blade gets little support from the sides of the kerf (the slot left in the material by the saw), and its flexibility can lead to wandering. Careful setting of the correctly chosen blade and the machine is essential if accurate work is to be achieved.

It is an unfortunate characteristic of many scrollsaw blades that they have a tendency to be 'biased' to left or right. If one pushes the material in a straight line at the blade to effect a straight cut, one has to

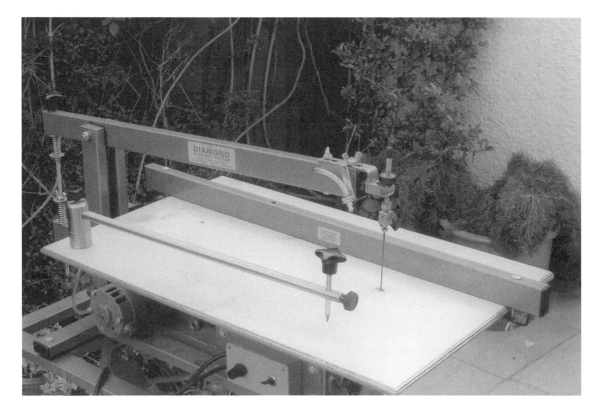

To the right of the blade can be seen the fence, clamped temporarily to the saw-table. To the left is a circle cutting attachment.

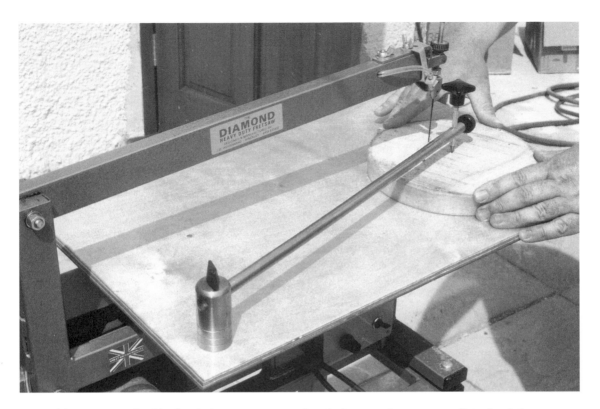

A roughly sawn circular blank is being resawn to make a hole to receive an expanding chuck for gripping on a lathe. This is an efficient way to produce the required hole. The accessory comprises the support column pivoted at the rear of the table, and a rod to carry the centre-pin that fixes in the workpiece centre. Infinite adjustment of the rod length and radius is available, plus height of the centre-pin to suit the thickness of the workpiece.

counteract the tendency for the cut to bear to one side or another. The use of a fence, or parallel saw-guide, is almost useless, being defeated by this tendency. At least the veering away from the central line is usually consistent, however, so all is not lost.

Apart from the fence supplied by the manufacturer, a simple arrangement may be set up with a piece of wood, about 50mm × 25mm (2in × 1in), to act as a fence. This may be clamped temporarily to the scrollsaw table. Before adding the wooden fence, it is essential to first carry out a simple experiment:

1. Choose, as a test-piece, a piece of scrap material about the same thickness as that selected for the job.
2. Scribe on it a centre-line making sure that it is parallel to the edges and place it touching the blade, as if in readiness for sawing.
3. Draw pencil lines on the table along each side, using the test-piece as a straight-edge.
4. Saw the test-piece following the centre-line, 'steering' it to ensure that the blade follows the line. Aim to 'split' the line.
5. After sawing, say, 50mm or 75mm

(2–3in), stop the machine and examine the set-up. Any 'veering' of the work-piece will be discernible by the difference between its edge and one of the prescribed lines on the table.

6. Draw lines either side of the test-piece, which may then be removed and discarded. This will show the angular position required for the fitting of a fence to ensure parallel cutting.

7. Set the blade of a sliding bevel to the saw-line relative to the angle of the leading edge of the saw-table. The sliding bevel may now be used as a reference for the setting of a fence for parallel sawing with this blade at this tension. Any variation in the set-up will probably need a repeat of the foregoing procedure to ensure parallel cutting.

If it is necessary to clamp accessories, such as a fence, or a lamp, like as not, the underside of a cast scrollsaw table will be uneven with raised webs as part of the design construction. Use double-sided adhesive tape to attach pads of wood to fill up the hollows. This will solve the problem of inadequate clamp-seating.

Lighting

Much of the work done by scrollsaw needs accurate attention to detail and therefore there is a need for a well-lit environment. Even better if the lighting is localized to illuminate the saw, best of all if it can pin-point the blade.

Some spotlights with angular adjustment come with clamps for fixing on tables or benches, but whilst admirable for general-purpose bench work, these take up too much space on the average saw-table. Best to site the spotlight, either by its clamp or on its stand, if it has one, on a workbench if it is near. Small quartz-halogen lamps provide excellent illumination and are ideal for this situation.

Hold-downs and Guards

Most people would consider the hold-down as a necessity rather than an accessory, and these are best if they incorporate a guard to protect fingers from accidentally touching the sawblade. Let us look at the functions separately.

The term 'hold-down' is itself a misnomer, in that there is no question that a 'hold' is being made by that component. Hold-downs are intended to prevent the tendency of the workpiece to rise with the upstroke of sawblade during the sawing action. Naturally, the teeth on the blade will have a certain amount of grab on the sides of the kerf, with the result that the workpiece will try to follow the blade on the upstroke.

With some scrollsaws, it is possible to set the action of the blade to describe an 'orbit', so-to-speak. In this case, the blade moves back very slightly on the up-stroke, a matter of a hair's-breadth, away from the sawn face. This reduces the drag on the upstroke and lessens the tendency to lift the workpiece. Most notable of the machines with this feature is the Diamond Heavy Duty Fretsaw.

Even with such possibilities, most users will feel more comfortable with a machine that has a positive hold-down, and these differ greatly in design, if not in functional principles. Primarily the height setting concerns the operator. Obviously, if the hold-down is in direct contact with the surface of the workpiece, it may bind and handicap its free movement horizontally. With the possibility of irregular thickness of the

Perhaps the last word in hold-downs is the toolbridge by Diamond, which comprises two independent feet, adjustable for height, radial and lateral position, together with a rear blade support. An alternative position for the dust-blower nozzle is available plus a magnifying lens on a universal joint for close work. Add a pair of super-fast blade-changers and the sawyer is ready for refined and rapid scrollsawing.

A combined hold-down and guard is a feature of this machine. It is made from transparent plastic and may be lifted quickly to permit access for blade changing.

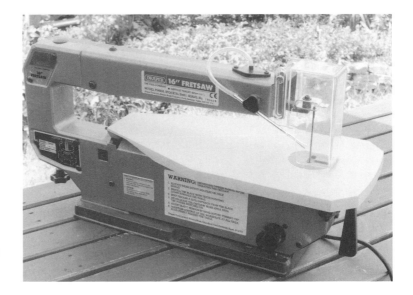

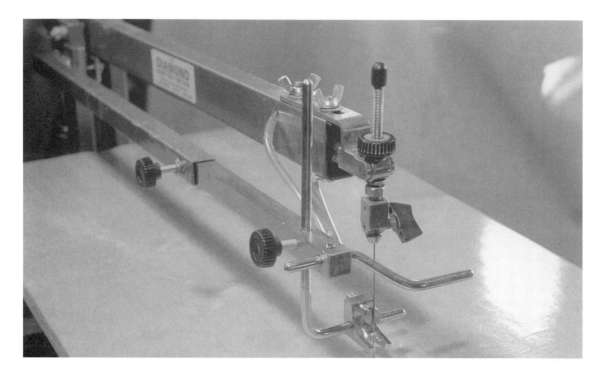

This hold-down is adjustable for distance and height with the refinement of a rear blade support to counter the tendency of blades, particularly slender ones, to buckle and bow under strain. It also has an adjustable guard in the form of the S-shaped bar inserted near the front end of the hold-down beam.

Another clever hold-down/guard is depicted here. No adjustment is necessary; pressure on the workpiece is exerted by a spring incorporated in its design.

42

workpiece this is a common problem, necessitating a careful inspection prior to commencing the sawing and setting the hold-down to clear the thickest part.

Some hold-downs are made of a cast metal, either iron or alloy, and often come with the need to fettle the surface or edges. Best to make sure the lower face, that comes into contact with the surface of the workpiece, is as clean and free from rough spots as possible, to aid the unhindered progress of the sawing.

The guard has an almost impossible task. It may at first sight seem simple to say its function is to prevent operators from accidentally cutting themselves during a sawing operation. It is probably unnecessary to point out that if the guard defended against any clumsy eventuality, it would probably enclose the blade sufficiently to render it impossible to cut materials either! Clearly, guards are therefore a compromise, some designs of which are more successful than others. The nearest to perfection are those made from transparent plastic, allowing visual contact whilst cutting and acting as hold-downs simultaneously. Draper and Rexon are good examples. However, handling of plastic materials inevitably means gradual deterioration of the surface, that leads to the eventual reduction in transparency. By careful cleaning using special techniques and Micro-mesh or other fine polishing materials, it may be possible to rejuvenate transparent guards.

A convenient accessory is the power take-off, seen here with a flexible drive connected (encased in the red cable cover). This may be used to power drill bits for perforating access holes in the workpiece, or other tools such as abrasive wheels for de-burring. The seat is a boon to the sawyer who has a hefty schedule of work, but it may be removed if large workpieces need space in which to swing. Attached to the bottom of the stand may be seen the footswitch, supported above the floor to prevent accidental activation.

> Reduce wear on the surfaces of see-through plastic hold-downs by fitting a small knob for handling when raising, lowering or adjusting.

Power Take-off

Some manufacturers offer a useful optional extra in the way of a power take-off that may be used to drive ancillary tools such as a flexible drive or a disc sander. Either of these are useful, the flexible drive for drilling blade-entry holes for aperture sawing and the disc sander for quick trimming of components.

Dust Extraction

Most machines have a port for coupling to a vacuum extractor; a domestic type will be suitable for the relatively small amount of dust generated by the scrollsaw blade. For the frequent user, however, it probably makes sense to use an extractor dedicated to collecting machine-made dust. If for no other reason than for health and safety, such efficiency makes sense. The bonus of a clean work area is also valuable, especially if precision is required. Most dust extractors are suitable for coupling to other machines either simultaneously or by transferring connections from one to another on a temporary basis. Costs of small extraction units suitable for the home workshop have reduced to an accessible level, little more than the cost of the domestic vacuum cleaner. The advantages of the dust extractor include much greater suction and a larger waste capacity.

5 Preparing and Maintaining the Scrollsaw

Before embarking on any serious work with the scrollsaw, it behoves the user to consider ways in which the machine may be brought to its best, or even improved.

In the contemporary world of mass-production, improvements made by manufacturers to increase productivity and maintain low-as-possible costs, may mean that short-cuts have to be made, causing some compromise on quality.

Take finish, for example. Most metal-work will be either plated or painted, and in the latter case, some parts may be bare if the finishing process was in some way at fault. No matter, as long as the machine is functioning correctly, since whilst a complaint to the supplier may result in an exchange of the machine, this will not happen without some inconvenience to the buyer. Good counsel might suggest minor corrective treatment by the new owner. In any case, from time to time maintenance of the painted surfaces may be necessary due to knocks and scratches usually suffered in consequence of moving the machine around from place to place, in which case a complete repaint should be considered.

A clean, wholesome appearance will keep the machine not only looking attractive but also encouraging to an enthusiastic operator. Fortunately, these machines are relatively small with few painted surfaces, so upkeep in this respect is not too great an undertaking.

Bearings

Other items might require a more critical and harder-to-please attitude. Consider the bearings; are they the correct type, and are they fitted correctly? A simple test to ascertain their efficiency is to take the arms and gently try to move them from side to side whilst the machine is stationary. There should not be the slightest movement, if all is as it should be. Any doubt about these important parts should be referred to the supplier immediately.

Saw-table

Whether the table be of plate steel, cast metal, or wood, its surface finish should be clean, flat and polished. Yes, polished. Look at the sole on any professional cabinet-maker's plane and, like as not, it will be 'as shiny as a shilling in a sweep's armpit', as an old saying goes. In other words, we speak not just about the desirability of a beautiful appearance of a treasured tool, but the lack of unnecessary friction.

An apprentice woodworker would probably have spent days refining a plane grinding away every superfluity from its sole. Using a piece of plate glass as a flat bed, with grinding paste and elbow-grease, the sole would be flattened and polished at the same time. A brand new tool would have been subjected to this treatment, straight from the packing.

Note, the standard wooden table has been removed to show the heavy metal sub-table. Beneath it to the left are the on–off switch and speed control. The footswitch overrides these, giving remote power and speed control.

Quite apart from the machining carried out during production, no doubt with all the precision available to the skilled machinist, there is the need to 'weather' castings, prior to machining them. In past times when labour and space were cheaper, castings were left to cure, out in the open, almost like the seasoning of timber. The longer they were left out, the better, so that any warping or twisting would have taken place; any discrepancies of alignment would then have been corrected by the machining process.

Nowadays, there is little likelihood of a casting receiving months of weathering to cure, so consequently some defects may be found in the cast saw-table. Fortunately, nothing like the precision of a plane-sole is required of a saw-table, with regard to flatness, however, the finish of the surface is just as critical.

Close examination of the new table will probably reveal circular marks, shallow grooves left by the surface grinder, and these will hold grime and grease, both detrimental to the smooth movement necessary for precise work-handling.

One method for improving the finish is as follows:

1. Remove the table from the machine. This is not essential, but it makes the process easier.
2. Clean up the surface with a degreasing agent of some sort.
3. With a flat sanding block, or an orbital sander, fitted with an emery paper (wet-or-dry works very well) of about 120 grit, proceed to cut back the whole surface until all signs of grinding are removed.
4. Repeat, with finer grades to about 500 grit.
5. Buff the surface with 0000 grade steel wool.

> From time to time, polish the saw-table surface with a proprietary brand of lanolin. This will preserve the finish and keep down the friction, without affecting the surface quality of the workpiece.

Table Inserts

It is usual to find the table recessed at the point where the saw blade passes through it. This is normally filled with a supplementary insert made from plastic or soft metal, circular in shape usually, with a slot to admit the blade. Its function is to provide close contact with the blade to support the workpiece during sawing.

All sawing operations, with whatever type of saw – band, circular, even handsaws – need support beneath the work and, up to a point, the closer the better. Plastics are used for renewable inserts to avoid damage to blade teeth and to preserve the table from wear.

In some cases, the insert as supplied is thinner than the recess in which it sits, meaning that the level of the table is higher than the insert. This defeats the purpose of the insert and helps to create vibration due to lack of solid contact. Generally, the problem is easily solved by applying packing, maybe a postcard or similar material, sufficient to bring the insert level with the table. Double-sided adhesive tape will retain the layers until renewal is necessary. Renewal may be by a duplicate part obtained from the manufacturer, or a shop-made copy. For the latter, a hardwood is fine for the job, easily made (on the scrollsaw, of course!). Try this:

1. Remove the blade from the scrollsaw.
2. Remove the worn or damaged insert.
3. Take a piece of thin card and place it over the recess in the table.
4. Tap the surface of the card gently, where it makes contact with the recess edges, using a small hammer.
5. Remove the card and, with a craft knife or sharp scissors, cut out the pattern made by the mark of the recess.
6. Prepare a piece of hardwood, or fibreboard of some sort, reducing the thickness to that of the depth of the recess, or if anything, leave it slightly thicker.
7. Mark out the shape of the recess on the prepared material using the card pattern.

Cut out the insert using a supplementary table. Trim the outer edge if necessary, to ensure a close fit to the periphery of the recess, and level off the surface of the insert flush with the table.

This method may be used to make an alternative insert, with a hole only slightly larger than the blade width, for the support of tiny workpieces. Self-made inserts may be slotted to facilitate quick changes.

Table Tilt

All of the scrollsaws available at present are equipped with tilting tables. This offers opportunities for cutting bevels and mitres and, you may be sure, opportunity for errors of setting! Compound mitres are also achievable with relative ease.

Whether adjusting for a bevel cut, or returning to a normal 90 degree arrangement, it is not wise to rely on the indicated angles on the protractor scales if attached to the tilting mechanism. Such scales must be regarded as a guide only, since because there are several components associated with the table tilting facility, there is potential for inaccuracy. Better to set the table at the indicated angle and check for errors on some scrap material, prior to launching into some magnum opus demanding great angular precision. Adjustment of the protractor scales, or the zero pointer, following verification of the table setting, is possible in some cases, thus helping subsequent angle modification.

We may also consider the possibilities of angular cutting for inlay work, such as marquetry, where, using the 'sandwich' method, pieces are cut with the table set at an angle less than 90 degrees. This allows inner pieces to fit into apertures and fill up the space created by the saw kerf (*see* Chapter 8 for more details).

Siting

It is worth going to some trouble to locate and fix the scrollsaw with the following considerations in mind.

Safety

Although aspects of safety are dealt with elsewhere in this book, they are referred to here as being essential to good practice.

Electricity supply must feature prominently here. For instance, even if a no-volt-release (NVR) switch is fitted, it makes sense to locate the machine near a mains socket, preferably switched if possible. This means that if and when any extraneous work is to be carried out, like the fitting of an accessory or when some mechanical adjustment may be needed, the machine can be isolated temporarily from the main electrical supply.

Accessibility

If there is the possibility of working pieces larger than the saw-table, make sure that there is sufficient space to swing the work freely without the danger of colliding with some obstruction near the machine.

Light

Whether relying on some source of natural light from a window or skylight, or from artificial illumination, lighting of the saw-table is crucial to the success of accurate cutting. Strong overhead light is desirable, with specific concentration on the blade. (Refer to Chapter 6 for more information.)

> If the light source is limited in strength or direction, use a mirror to redirect it.

Lubrication

Manuals usually include helpful information about the lubrication of the moving parts on the scrollsaw. If however, the machine was acquired second-hand, or the handbooks are lost, it should be a simple matter to locate the moving parts by a careful examination of the machine. A few drops of machine lubricant, commonly available at any hardware store, should be applied to these points on a regular basis, say once a month for a machine used frequently. It does no harm to use a cleaning fluid prior to the oil, to effect a flushing out of grit and dust.

In the case of a hard-worked scrollsaw, an annual 'spring-clean' should be undertaken, by a knowledgeable person, involving a general strip-down of the dismantleable components for inspection, cleaning and lubrication. Reassembly of the machine to return it to its former efficiency requires care and experience, and is not to be taken lightly or experimentally.

So called 'sealed-for-life' bearings mean sealed for the life of the bearing, and not the operator! Hopefully, the operator will outlive the bearings, with the result that in time replacement becomes a necessity. Excessive vibration may indicate this condition, particularly if it worsens gradually. Replacement should be carried out after consultation with the manufacturer or a skilled mechanical engineer with experience of scrollsaw machinery.

Some operating mechanisms include springs, hard-worked components opening and closing each time the frame reciprocates. These should be included in the lubrication schedule, particularly if the coils come together completely in the operation; not to forget the points at which they are anchored.

A 'Finger' Fence

Many years ago, I learned a trick for cutting parallel pieces on a scrollsaw. It was in fact a method used for cutting veneers on a bandsaw, but the principle is similar.

Take a piece of hardwood sufficient in length to reach from the edge of the saw table to the blade, wide enough to be gripped with a clamp and about 25mm (1in) high.

At the end to be used as the 'finger-fence', taper it in width to a radiused point, say 3mm (⅛in). The whole unit is then clamped to the table with its point set from the saw-blade at whatever width is required of the workpiece. A mark is made for visual reference on the workpiece, preferably with a marking-gauge, or a marking knife with a straight-edge. The edge of the workpiece is then brought to bear against the fence-point.

As the sawing proceeds, any tendency to deviate is easily counteracted by maintaining contact with the finger-fence point and 'steering' the workpiece to keep the blade cutting along the marked line. It is possible to achieve accurate parallel cutting of relatively long pieces down to veneer thickness using this method.

Here the 'finger' fence has been set at a short distance from the blade and immediately to the side of, and level with, the teeth.

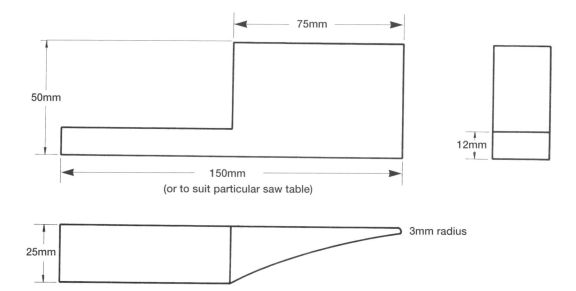

Fig. 18 Details of the finger fence.

In this example, the workpiece has a profiled edge that is bearing against the fence to produce a parallel slice. Consistent thickness can be produced using this method, in either curved or straight cutting.

SAFETY AT WORK

Most machines are potentially dangerous. Scrollsaws are no exception to this rule, but fortunately to a lesser degree than most. It is worth mentioning that, in hindsight, most 'accidents' may be seen to have been avoidable. Here are guide lines to reduce the associated risks and increase efficiency simultaneously.

First Step

Always read the instruction book supplied by the manufacturer, taking special note of specifications, capacities and warnings.

Electricity

Many machines are supplied with plugs already fitted and one hopes that the intentions of the manufacturer to comply with regulations are upheld by delivery to the appropriate destination. It can be somewhat irksome to discover that the plug that has been fitted is suitable only for connecting to some foreign system!

Follow this check-list:
1. Ensure that the voltage setting on the machine corresponds to that of the local mains supply.
2. Check, where applicable, that the fuses fitted in the circuit are in accordance with the manufacturer's specification.
3. See that correct cables are connected to correct terminals.
4. Inspect all electrical connections, making sure that terminals are secure.
5. Whenever major adjustments or dismantling of parts of the machine are undertaken, disconnect the machine from mains supply, by removing the plug, not just by switching off.

Bench, or Support

Use the machine within the capacities stipulated by the manufacturer.

Whether the machine is to be free-standing or mounted on a bench, it is imperative that the support be stable and secure. Immobility is the order of the day when it comes to the body of any machine – this is not simply for the sake of safety, but for accurate operation.

Check that the machine will not move when pressure is applied to the blade during a sawing operation. Despite the relatively lightweight nature of the work associated with scrollsawing, in certain sawing situations pressures may be considerable. If, for instance, a hardwood workpiece of 50mm (2in) thickness is being sawn on a lightweight bench model, the machine may well move unless it is fixed, either permanently with bolts, or temporarily with clamps.

Dust

Sawing produces dust, and in the case of the scrollsaw, the dust is fine and powdery, light enough to become airborne at the slightest movement of air. Unfortunately, the machines that come with a dust blower fitted do not remove the dust, they simply keep the cutting area clear for visual control, during the process of which, dust becomes airborne and flows towards the operator.

Inhaling dust is obviously to be avoided if possible, and there are several methods of achieving this:
1. By wearing a mask for covering the nose and mouth. This can be a simple, paper-based product, purchasable for small sums from most hardware stores. Elasticated straps retain the mask.

2. By wearing a respirator. Some of the recently developed types are not heavy, and supply fresh air via a filter. The eyes are also protected by the transparent visor.
3. By removing the dust at source by suction. This can be by means of an extractor or vacuum cleaner, and is best used in combination with either of the above. At its best, it should be large enough to have the power to draw away the particles of dust as they are produced, and small enough to be conveniently sited without interfering with the sawing operation.

Guards

Opinions differ as to what constitutes an efficient guard and, often as not, guards are intended to reduce the risk of, or prevent, fingers touching the saw blade.

Often as not, the more effective the guard, the more obstructive it is likely to be to movement of fingers and thus to freedom of manipulation of the workpiece, particularly if the latter is small enough to require contact close to the blade.

Some guards are combined with a hold-down, thus preventing fingers coming into contact with the moving blade, whilst reducing the tendency for, or preventing, lifting of the workpiece during sawing. Such guards fall into two categories: those made of metal, with a partial barring of the access to the blade and those made of transparent plastic, which virtually enclose the blade. Unfortunately the latter often tend to distort the view slightly, or worse, in time, become scratched with use and obscure the view.

The Hold-down

There is a natural tendency with most machines for the work to rise from the table as the blade rises. To counteract this, many machines are supplied with a hold-down. This is an attachment fitted to a fixed arm, independent of the saw frame, permitting adjustment of its height and location. Its purpose is to prevent the lifting of the workpiece during sawing; in some models, a guard is incorporated in the design, to prevent accidental contact of the fingers with the moving blade.

It is wise to use this device whenever possible until the knack is achieved of holding and guiding simultaneously. Sometimes, if the work is very small, it is not possible to apply the hold-down, in which case, refer to Chapter 8.

Footswitch

If small pieces, or for that matter any-sized pieces, are being sawn, the advantages of a foot-switch to both power and stop the machine are many. Being able to bring both hands to hold and guide the workpiece is the obvious one, plus the facility to stop and recommence during an incomplete cutting operation.

Seating

Whilst not essential, it makes sense to sit during lengthy work programmes, for reasons of comfort, concentration and physical assurance. There is no better way of tackling a job that requires consistent accuracy than to be poised, alert and secure. A chair with good back support at a height to allow the forearms to move horizontally, similar to those used by typists, will be an enormous asset.

Lighting

Needless to say, without sufficient lighting, faults are likely to occur, not only with the execution of the cutting but with reduced control of the placing of the hands relative to the sawblade due to impaired visibility. Thus, the possibility of inaccuracies cannot be ruled out, moreover, accidents involving fingers and sawblades may occur.

Apart from an adequate main overhead light, an auxiliary light on an adjustable stem is important, to allow its placing for maximum lightspread for localized illumination, with minimum inconvenience to the user.

Operational Care

Placing of the fingers when guiding workpieces during sawing needs awareness at several levels. Initially, one considers the moving upper arm as a potential finger-squasher and light-basher! Before switching on the machine, check that all fingers and equipment are clear of the frame.

Remember, whilst it is true that the scrollsaw is much more sympathetic to careless fingers than would be a bandsaw or circular saw, it is best not to put it to the test! Keep the fingers to the side or rear of the serrated front edge of the blade, taking extra care when cutting curves and corners.

A modern machine with electronic speed control and an LED digital read-out indicating the operating speed in strokes per minute. Being an American import operating on a lower-voltage, a transformer is required to power it in Europe or the United Kingdom. Normally the machine is supplied complete with the transformer unit, seen here alongside.

6 Organizing the Workshop

Few people are able to choose their working environment unless they are involved professionally in woodwork of some sort, or are wealthy amateurs. Most are stuck with a shed in the garden, a space in the basement, a converted garage or occasional use of the kitchen table.

As long as there is adequate space to cope with the essential equipment, the type of venue is not important. One of the disadvantages of the temporary workshop, as in the case of the kitchen table or a portion of a living room, is the probability that the space needs to be cleared up at the end of the work session. This tends to create a hiatus in the procedure, and may of course be counter-productive in creative terms.

Whichever it happens to be, many of the same principles apply to all. For instance, sufficient light must fall on the workplace, by natural light from a window during the day, or strategically placed electric light for night or winter time.

Lighting

Examining the question of light first of all; consider the use of small spotlights on adjustable stems. These are fine, providing their stands are not so large that they create obstacles to hinder the movement of the hands or the workpiece. Happy the person who has a saw that incorporates a bracket or lamp-holding facility.

Siting of the light source is crucial, and some time spent in experiment will be worthwhile. Location of the light behind the saw blade will almost certainly project a shadow forward to clash with or partially obscure the saw-line, if marked on the workpiece, causing potential inaccuracy, or at least some insecurity. If positioned on either side of the blade, although a shadow of the blade is cast, it probably will not distract from the marked saw-line. The ideal would be a siting of the lamp as near to the operator as possible, shielded suitably from the eye and directed towards the blade. Even so, it is difficult to avoid contact with the lighting equipment.

My last workshop had the luxury of a glazed roof, was north-facing, and had consistent natural illumination during daylight hours. I am already planning changes in my present workshop to duplicate that superb condition.

Blade Storage

It is surprising how much space is required to store the ancillary equipment associated with the scrollsaw.

Take blades for instance. Some thoughtful manufacturers incorporate in the design of the machine such things as a blade box, to house spare blades. If no convenient holder is attached, then some other receptacle should be used to obviate frustration when changing or selecting blades. Often as not, blades are supplied in plastic envelopes, but unfortunately most of these packages need to be partly destroyed in order to remove the blades, rendering them useless as secure receptacles thereafter. A few suppliers provide blades in a more durable wallet.

The problem of blade storage is partly due to the fact that a wide range is necessary, accompanied by the fact that the blades themselves are not quickly identified by eye. This necessitates creating some special storage facility to hold the collection with a clear labelling system to ease the problem of selecting and returning blades after use. Probably the quickest retrieval system coupled with tidiness is one of the proprietary magnetic strips used for tool retention, available from hardware shops and tool merchants. Add a label to sectionalize the different varieties separated with rubber bands, and a potential source of frustration and time-wasting is eliminated.

Tool Storage

Many small tools are needed to complete the collection of ancillary equipment associated with the scrollsaw. Here is my own list, some used frequently, others rarely, but from time to time they are all needed and the ability to find them when required is essential if my equanimity is to be retained: small tenon saw, pliers, pincers, rule, craft knives, marking gauge, clamps, engineer's combination square, block plane, chisels, sanding block, selection of drill bits, safety glasses, dust mask, bodkins, tweezers.

Most of these will fit into any small tool-cabinet or shelf system, and so much the better if this is within easy reach of the scrollsaw location. Underneath the machine is fine, providing that dust from the saw is deflected from falling into the storage area, or preferably, is drawn away by vacuum extraction.

Raw Material Storage

Fortunately, much of the raw material of the scroll-saw user, whether wood, metal or plastics, is usually relatively small. In fact, a raid on the local timber merchant's off-cut box in exchange for a little cash should result not only in bargains, but a useful mixed bag of goods. Often, what one man rejects may represent a treasure to another.

Even so, the material has to be stored, preferably in a dry, clean environment that is readily accessible. If the whole stock can be seen at a glance, even better.

For sheet materials less than 150mm (6in) sq., any chest of drawers or shelving system will suffice, but stuff over the size of the average book is a different matter. Obviously if the sheets are laid flat, it is difficult to find a particular piece, it is difficult to see quickly what the extent of present stock is and, what is worse, valuable floor space is being used. This latter, flat space, is always a premium in small workshops. A vertical storage system is one answer.

Using standard plastic pipe used for domestic water plumbing, a cheap and effective racking may be built to whatever size is required to suit the individual needs. Many connectors, of various angles, are available to construct one's own custom rack. If narrow pieces are racked end-on, that is at right angles to the wall and wider pieces racked flat with their faces parallel to the wall, then space is better utilized. If large sheets or large quantities are to be kept, then obviously something stronger would be necessary, in which case metal piping could be used in the same way.

7 Materials

WOOD

Wood is the most obvious material to come to mind for scrollsaw use. It is, of course, only one of many, but in itself it covers a wide range.

Solid Timbers

Either in veneer form, as thin as card, or plank as thick as a refectory table, cutting solid wood is a natural task of the scrollsaw. Density plays a big part in the choice of suitable woods, some theoretically 'soft' woods can be fibrous and tough, leaving a fluffy finish on cut sides. Others categorized as hardwoods may have a consistent, regular grain that cuts cleanly and smoothly. Individual pieces vary anyway, so it should surprise no-one to discover that just when a timber is known and understood, along comes a renegade which does not conform. Well, that is the nature of Nature…

Prime consideration after having decided on the variety of timber and the dimensions of a particular workpiece, must be the grain structure. The same applies to any other kind of timber application if structural factors are involved. If, however, the intentions are to create decorative or artistic pieces, the parameters are primarily concerned with appearance.

Veneer

Two basic types of veneer are available in general: 'sawn' and 'peeled'. The former type probably speaks for itself in that it is produced by sawing; it comes in sheets around 1mm (about 0.040in) in thickness. Hardwood that does not lend itself to the peeling process is usually supplied in this form.

Peeled veneer is cut by applying a knife to a revolving cylindrical log, in the manner of a gigantic pencil-sharpener. Veneer produced in this way comes in thicknesses around 0.6mm (0.025in). Naturally, the peeled variety is fragile, due to its thin section and the tendency for splits to run with the grain.

> If splits are occurring very frequently during the working of a particular veneer, try dampening the surface with a moist cloth just before sawing.

Plywoods

Sheets of plywood are made up of several veneers bonded together. The grain direction is an important consideration in its make-up, since the intention is to lay each veneer at right angles to its neighbour. Since the grain of the outer veneers of plywood panels always run in the same direction, it follows that the board must be made up of an odd number of layers; 3, 5, 7, 9, etc.

Sizes of boards are given by stating the first dimension along which the grain runs. So, if a sheet is stated to measure, say 1220 × 610mm (48 × 24in) this means that the grain runs in the direction of the longer side. If on the other hand the board size is given as 610 × 1220mm (24 × 48in), then the grain will run with the shorter side.

Apart from plywoods of less than 3mm (⅛in) thick, used for hobbies and model-makers, thicknesses are available in increments of 1mm up to 25mm (1in). Smaller thicknesses are usually made of three-ply, and more than five-ply is referred to as multi-ply.

Scrollsaws can cope easily with any thickness of ply, even up to the thickest, and inasmuch as materials differ in the manufacture of this material, so blades must be selected accordingly. Multi-ply sheets contain more bonding resin, because they have more joints, meaning that a harder blade will be needed.

Some facing veneers are hard one side, soft on the other. Some sheets are the same both sides. Qualities vary in the same manner. This may matter where projects are seen one or both sides.

MDF

Of course, traditionalists will always prefer to use natural timber, if only for its appearance – who wouldn't? But medium-density fibreboard, or for that matter,

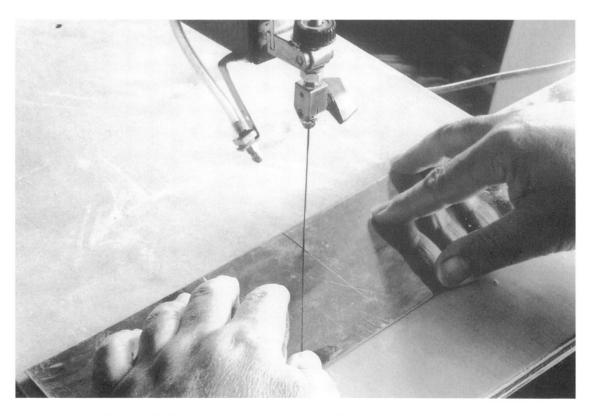

A piece of 3mm (⅛in) steel is being cut with a metal-cutting blade running at a relatively slow speed.

low- and high-density fibreboards, may all be used quite satisfactorily on the scroll-saw. In fact for some purposes, MDF cannot be equalled.

When cutting through the thickness of MDF boards, unlike plywoods or indeed solid wood, no voids will be revealed, and whether cutting in curves or diagonals, no irregularities of grain will affect the cutting or the finish.

Thicknesses from 3mm (⅛in) up to 50mm (2in) are available. MDF is also excellent for use as a substrate for veneering.

Plastics

Many varieties of plastic sheet are viable as suitable materials for scrollsaw work. Whether it is of the hard sort, like some of the acrylics, or soft, such as the polythenes, will affect the choice of blade and speed, as in the case of wood. However, as a general rule, choose a speed half that used for wood, with a moderately coarse tooth structure and a moderate feed. The object is to avoid splitting if the material is brittle, and to avoid burning if less hard. It is possible for the plastic to weld itself together after the saw has passed through,

leaving a fused path behind the blade; this is an obvious sign of the generation of too much heat.

Metals

Metal cutting blades are advised for hard metals, and obviously for softer metals too. However, the latter may be sawn with normal wood cutting blades, with some reduction in effective life. Slow speeds and fine teeth for thin sheet is advisable, plus a little oil to lubricate and cool the blade and workpiece. If the machine has a stroke adjustment it is better to use it in short stroke mode.

Aluminium, copper and the associated alloys may be approached as for dense hardwood. Iron and steel need the best quality blades, produced especially for the purpose, coupled with stroke speeds down in the low hundreds.

> If hard brass is proving difficult to cut, anneal it and try again. Heat the brass to a dull red and allow it to cool slowly.

8 Making It Work

Since this book is concerned with the application of techniques of scrollsaw operation, I will dispense with definitions of the names given to the many ways that the machine may be used to decorate or create objects. Several chapters could be devoted to the etymology of terms such as marquetry, inlay, encrustation, intarsia, and so on. In the near future, I have the intention to produce a book of projects of many kinds using the scrollsaw in the various methods described herein. For the time being, however, I hope that this book serves as an introduction to the various parameters of the subject whose horizons may be extended.

The name, 'scrollsaw', may need clarification to some craftsmen who, on being confronted by one, might identify it as a 'fretsaw', correctly so. Both names are applicable to this type of machine, though it probably became known as the 'scrollsaw' in its progress from the hand-held variety to its mechanization. The term 'scroll', apart from the original reference to a roll of parchment, meant a line or form of some convoluted sculpture or ornament. No doubt it received its name due to its potential for negotiating the most complex of spirals.

There are some who might suggest that the hand-operated traditional fretsaw is capable of more refined work than the motorized types, and those with experience of both would probably agree. Nonetheless, its versatility, speed of operation and capacity for producing a greater

volume of work sets the motorized scrollsaw well aside from its hand-driven cousin. Let us accept there is a genuine need for both.

Basically, as elaborated upon elsewhere in this book, the motorized scrollsaw is comprised of a C-shaped frame holding a slender saw blade between its open ends. A rotary movement, supplied by a motor, is converted by a mechanical function causing the frame to reciprocate and produce vertical movement of the blade.

For those new to the scrollsaw, it is useful to think of the saw-blade as a type of drill, piercing the material as it descends vertically. Since the cross-section of a blade is rectangular, cutting only on its thin, leading edge, it follows that only forward movement of the workpiece will result in successful sawing. This may seem an obvious statement, however, I have seen many new to the scrollsaw attempting to push the workpiece sideways against the flat of the blade. This usually happens when the operator is 'losing the line', that is, when the saw has been allowed to drift away from the marked line.

The fundamental requirement, to feed the workpiece towards the blade whilst 'steering' it to bring the marked line in contact with the front edge of the blade, is paramount to the success of all sawing operations on this type of machine. It may help to compare the blade of the scrollsaw with that of the bandsaw; obviously the bandsaw blade is much wider and thicker and therefore any attempt to move the workpiece sideways or across the blade would result in resistance and little effective cutting. Continued lateral pressure, what is more, could result in blade damage or even breakage. Similar comments apply to the scrollsaw blade; the fact that it is smaller should exemplify even more the inefficiency of movements other than forward against the front edge of the blade.

BSF – The Golden Rule

Remember it as **B**est **S**awing **F**undamentals:

B = blade; S = speed; F = feed.

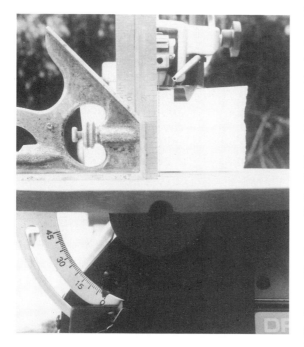

Setting the saw blade to cut vertically should present no problem. Checking by eye, with an engineer's square, and adjusting the table is the first step. As may be seen here, it was necessary to adjust the pointer on the protractor scale on the machine to register on the zero after the correction was made to the table setting.

Some elaboration is due. This is a simple reference to considerations of the desirable balancing of the three ingredients of successful scroll-sawing. Having decided upon the appropriate material, its necessary thickness and profile of sawing, the relevant blade is selected. Some guidance on blades may be obtained from Chapter 3.

This is then linked to the speed, that is the speed of the stroke of the reciprocating blade, and the feed, or the rate at which the saw is fed into the work.

Stroke speed can be readily experimented with if the machine has an adjustable speed control, if on the other hand the machine has only one speed, the feed rate must be balanced with blade type.

Hard and fast rules are impossible, due to the diversity of material density and the varying 'feel' of the cutting experience from one sawyer to another. The tangible 'correctness' of this BSF balance is subjective and flexible but it undoubtedly exists for every individual.

Practice, using the projects later in this book as exercises, will help to develop good techniques. It is useful to study the given examples and copy the patterns several times, with the intention of repeating them.

Cross-cutting in a Straight Line

Cross-cutting is the term used for sawing across the grain. In itself it is one of the most common cuts in woodwork, and should present no problem to the scroll-sawyer, providing that it is understood that the two sides of the blade are not identical. To the naked eye it is almost impossible to see the 'set' or sharpness of the teeth. Under magnification, however, it would be seen that one side has a slightly wider set.

After cutting a sample block for test purposes, it was checked again with the square before continuing.

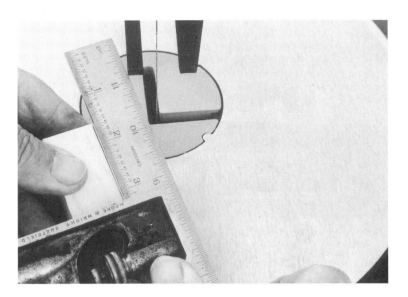

It is possible with great skill, to doctor the teeth with a fine abrasive stone to correct this condition, but it is very easy for the unwary to ruin the blade in the attempt.

What is required is to steer the blade along the line, and not simply to thrust the workpiece forward, expecting the saw cut to be parallel with the sides of the saw table. (Assuming the latter to have straight sides.) This may well mean that the direction of the movement of the workpiece may be at a diagonal, to compensate for this deficiency. The first time this is encountered may seem strange to the beginner, or to those experienced with other larger machines, though the same problem is often found on bandsaws. There is no need for alarm; all you do is simply follow the line and forget any extraneous references.

Rip-sawing in a Straight Line

Similar considerations are given to ripping along the grain as for the above comments on cross-cutting. However, there is a fundamental difference; rarely is grain truly straight, meaning that when following a line drawn along the grain occasionally the grain will be crossed at a slight diagonal. The transition from hard to soft grain, or vice versa, is where the trouble lies. The inconsistency makes it difficult to control the accuracy of the following of the line. In the case of cross-cutting, although the transition is discernible by differing pressures transmitted through the blade as it encounters different densities, this is met at right angles and does not contribute to a tendency to veer. When ripping, there is the complexity of bias to one side of the blade, as explained above, plus the potential to deviate diagonally due to the grain pattern. In this instance, use as strong a blade as possible, combined with a fast stroke speed and slow feed rate. Decrease the stroke speed and/or increase the feed rate if burning of the workpiece occurs.

Diagonal Sawing in a Straight Line

This can be the worst scenario when the previous two examples are considered, but

61

don't be discouraged, be prepared. Using exactly the same technique as for ripping, that of a strong blade with fast stroke and slow feed, follow the line and forget any other visual reference. At least there is comparatively more of each density from hard to soft grain at a diagonal making it easier to judge different densities.

Cutting Curves and Circles

Having read the foregoing about the potential hazards in cutting straight lines, one might assume that curves must combine all of the difficulties mentioned, plus more. Strangely enough, it is not so in practice, as any scroll-sawyer will relate. Providing that the correct balance of blade, speed and feed are faithfully applied, curves and circles will be the easiest lines to follow.

'Leaving' or 'Splitting' Lines

Developing the techniques for either 'leaving the line' or 'splitting the line' is essential for precise sawing. To explain this further: to 'leave the line' simply means to saw alongside the line in order to 'leave' it on one side, usually the required piece, thus the line remains a visible reference for sizing. This presumes that the adjacent part is either waste, or not required. Practice is recommended in the technique to leave the line on either left or right of the blade, since both are needed from time to time.

In the case of 'splitting the line', there is obviously a prerequisite to draw a line thick enough to permit the saw-blade to divide it between the two parts, leaving an equal amount of line on either part. This is particularly useful if adjacent pieces are needed for precision work such as

mechanical components or delicate filigree with geometrical motifs. Examples of each type are given in the projects section.

Cutting Small Pieces

When sawing pieces smaller than, say, a postage stamp, it may not be practicable to use a hold-down, and the fingers will then need to perform both the job of guiding the workpiece and holding it down.

The clue to successful sawing in this situation is in the term 'hold-down'. This is only possible if there is, in the immediate proximity of the blade, support for the workpiece – somewhat obvious, some may say, but often one sees the blade-hole so badly worn as to permit small pieces to slip through and disappear altogether!

Clearly, there is a need to maintain the supporting area around the blade hole and fortunately, tables usually are supplied with renewable inserts that fit flush with the table surface in a corresponding recess. These may be replaced when worn. Even the table inserts that are commonly supplied and fitted by the manufacturer may contain apertures too wide to support small stuff.

So, it may be necessary to use a supplementary 'table' with an access hole only slightly larger than the blade, permitting full support of the sawn edges of the workpiece during sawing. A trick used on bandsaw and circular saws when blade apertures become worn is as follows. A temporary 'table' may be applied, by simply passing a piece of scrap, lightweight, ply onto the table and entering the saw blade part-way into it. This may then be used as a support for small pieces.

Alternatively, a replacement insert may be used which is made of material of the correct thickness to come flush with the table surface, with a smaller than usual blade-hole. This may not always be practical, however, due to the difficulty in acquiring the correct material (*see* Chapter 6).

> A thimble is useful to protect the fingers, should they accidentally touch the moving blade, if sawing small pieces without the hold-down.

Cutting Larger Pieces

For this we may need to take a sideways glance at throat depth. Some machines

have the facility, if cuts are going to be long and straight, to rotate the blade position by 90 degrees, allowing the workpiece to pass sideways across the machine. An alternative trick is to take a pair of pliers and, holding the blade close to the holder, twist the blade through 90 degrees. Obviously, do the same at each end and, in effect, this will achieve a sideways cutting action.

Cutting Bevels

Most saw tables are tiltable, usually one way, up to 45 degrees. Some tilt both ways. Whichever; the tilting action pivots immediately below the table and in vertical

In the case of a scrollsaw with a tilting table but no protractor, it is a simple matter to adjust for bevel cutting, by the method shown above. An ordinary transparent protractor is held in front of the blade with the zero/90 line intersecting with the datum/blade line. The table is then adjusted according to the desired angle registering with the alignment of the blade. It is as well to use a protractor anyway, if accuracy is essential, rather than rely on the protractor scale on the machine.

alignment with the blade. If the table is lowered on the left of the blade, (the most common function) it follows that the right hand side of the table rises by the equal and opposite angle.

This facility of the angular disposition of the table relative to the saw blade, enables, for example, the cutting of mitres as used in picture frames, boxes and the like. Some experiment is necessary to achieve accuracy, regardless of the angles required, if joints are to look good. When sawing material over 25mm (1in) thick, it is best to use as wide a blade as possible, to counteract the tendency to flex. Setting over the table to 45 degrees, for example, means the cutting depth is increased to over 35mm (1⅜in).

Apart from jointing mitres, there are several other uses for angular cutting. One of these is sawing bevels on edges or apertures. This has the effect of attractively ornamenting what could be an otherwise ordinary object. See the House Number Plate and Gothic Mirror, in the projects section.

Hairpin Bends

Small radius cutting requires practice, in order to achieve an unbroken line – smooth, continuous travel coupled with a watchful attention to the exact following of the blade along the line. Most often the beginner under-compensates for the saw's ability to cut on small radii (less than 3mm (⅛in), resulting in an ever-widening spiral away from the line that is unrecoverable. Remember that the blade can only swivel in the gap made by its own teeth. Therefore there is a limit to the effective minimum radius achievable by any saw blade, dependant on the difference between the sawn kerf and the blade width.

Sharp Corners

Where sharp corners or on-the-spot-turns are needed, there is a technique that can be learned quickly, given some practice. If the blade has entered the workpiece to a point at which it is necessary to return or make a sharp turn, bear in mind that the back of the blade is plain and will not damage the material unless great pressure is applied. So, release the pressure on the toothed edge of the saw blade and using the back edge of the blade as a bearing, it is possible to swing the workpiece around, to recommence sawing at any other angle. A full 360 degree rotation is possible. It is an essential trick to master, and providing that the technique is understood and a disciplined course of practice is embarked upon, it will become a great asset. Try cutting triangles as an example.

Cutting Marquetry Packs

Marquetry is a specialized subject worthy of several volumes all to itself. Indeed many such already exist, but here is a brief introduction to one particular aspect of the craft, to exemplify another facet of this versatile machine.

Scrollsawing is one of many ways of cutting the intricate parts that comprise a marquetry picture. The 'pack', 'stack' or 'sandwich' system is the method associated with this type of work and may include metals, tortoiseshell, mother-of-pearl and other precious materials inlaid in, or laid on, a wooden base. The encrustation is used to adorn fine furniture and panelling. One of the founders of this method was André Charles Boulle; a college of fine woodworking still bears his name in Paris.

Principally, a pack of veneers less than 1mm (½₂in) thick are cut simultaneously.

Two veneers are taped together to form a pack. For the sake of the exercise the lower one is dark and the upper one is pale in colour. The direction of the grain is opposed.

A design is marked on the upper sheet and a hole made with a bodkin is used to perforate one of the corners. The bodkin is made from a wooden handle drilled to take a needle that is glued in place with epoxy resin. Access for a fine blade of 0.29mm (0.012in) is made this way.

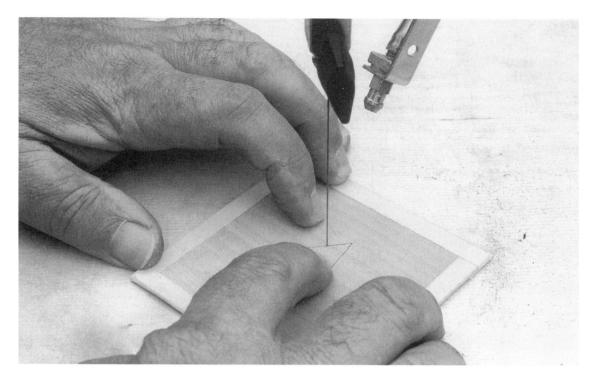

A low speed of around 150 s.p.m. is set and a gentle feed is maintained.
Care is taken on the sharp corners.

After the sawing is completed,
the tape is removed and the
inner triangles are placed in
opposite outer grounds. This
gives a typical 'Boulle' result,
with a gap around the designs
to be filled with a contrasting
coloured paste to emphasize
the outline. Several sheets
could be cut this way, to reduce
the cutting time for each motif.

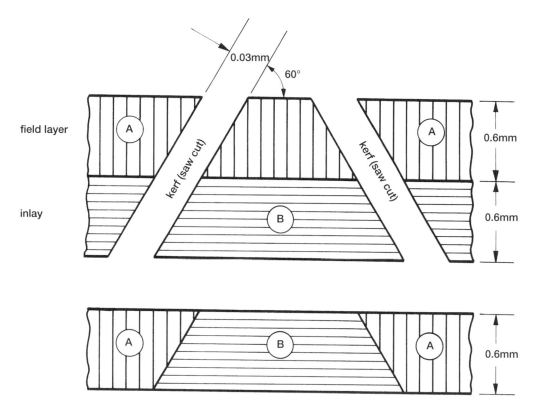

field layer

inlay

0.03mm

60°

kerf (saw cut)

kerf (saw cut)

A

A

B

0.6mm

0.6mm

A

B

A

0.6mm

Fig. 19 Diagrammatic view of the simultaneous cutting of two layers. The intention is to fit the lower piece, B, into the aperture in A leaving no gaps. The inner part of A and the outer part of B will therefore be wasted. The table is set at a much steeper angle to achieve this than is so in the example shown in Fig. 20.

A similar approach is by using four sheets, but this time the second and fourth are for waste. The first and third (from the top) are arranged with opposing grain and of contrasting colour. As in the previous example, the pack is retained by taping and a bodkin used to pierce an access hole for the blade.

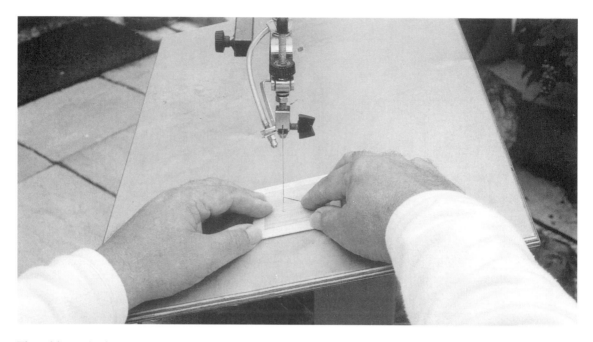

The table is tilted at 15 degrees for this cutting, and since the pack is made up of four layers, without adhesive to hold them as a solid, it is necessary to support the work close to the blade to prevent the upper layers rising and splitting. A refined hold-down as detailed in the illustration on page 41 would be more secure, but it does no harm to develop manual skills as an adjunct to the operation of the machine.

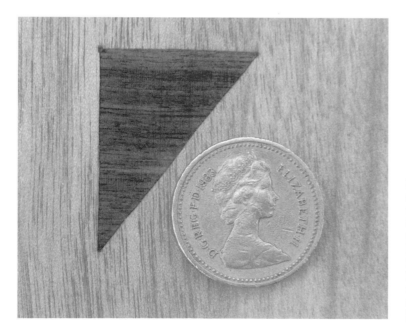

Separating the sawn pack, the second and fourth layers are discarded. The inner triangle of the third layer is inserted into the outer ground of the top layer. No gaps are visible and the access hole at the corner is barely the size of the hole in the number nine in the date stamped on the coin, shown here in enlargement.

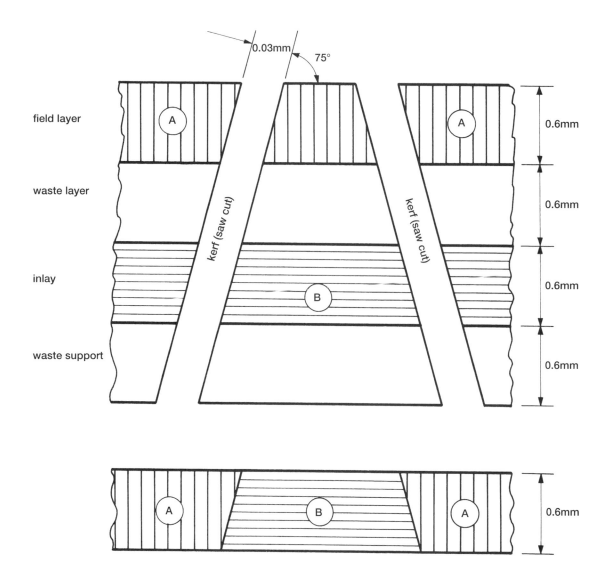

Fig. 20 Here is an example of angular cutting through four layers. A cleaner cut is obtained due to supporting waste layers and the table setting ensures a perfect, gapless fit of insert B into aperture A.

This means that the various portions from each layer of different woods or materials, may be interchanged to give a decorative effect. If the saw blade was operating vertically, there would be a gap around each portion where material was removed by the saw. Boulle emphasized this gap by filling it with coloured paste, thus creating a fine line around each motif. The technique allows many layers to be cut simultaneously, producing a vast amount of varied marquetry pieces.

A variation on this method, less productive but many would say superior, is that of cutting a pack of as few as two veneers, but with the saw-table set at an angle. The motifs can then be separated and since the lower one is tapered in its thickness, and matches the angle in the upper aperture, it fits without any gap, provided the table was set at the correct angle. No trial and error is involved, as long as the operator is prepared to draw a simple scale diagram, using known thicknesses of the materials and the blade, to determine the angle required. See the example illustrated in Fig. 19.

Cutting Intarsia

For the sake of brevity I am accepting that 'intarsia' is the current term referring to the craft of preparing and assembling adjacent pieces of material to make up a pictorial motif, after the manner of mosaic or marquetry. However, the material used is thick enough to be carved in relief giving the illusion of greater depth and, frequently, three dimensions. The picture or pattern is glued on, or inset into a ground, or backing.

A simple example would be to take the technique of cutting marquetry packs, described above, but working with a material thickness of between 6 and 12mm (¼–½in). The extra thickness permits a certain amount of carving to model the pieces to give a three-dimensional effect. An alternative method is to cut separate pieces traced from a pattern and then assembled on a backing. Obviously, skill in the preparation of the templates and the carving of the individual pieces is an essential requirement. There are excellent examples of this kind of work, all too often evidencing great skill with technical application – sadly, without the desirable inclusion of artistic ability. But that is another matter. At its best, intarsia is a wonderful way of presenting wood as an art medium.

9 Gallery

This chapter looks at examples of scrollsaw work by contemporary craftsmen. Each uses the scrollsaw in a distinct manner, for a different purpose and perhaps imparting something of their own character into their creations.

One of the best known of marquetry artists is Giovanni Aversa, an Italian now residing in Bristol whose work adorns many exquisite panels and objects. The charming trinket box pictured below is composed of at least a dozen pieces. The lid of the box is approximately 100×75mm (4×3in). Giovanni uses an Italian-made customized machine for his work as seen in the photograph overleaf.

A trinket box by marquetry artist Giovanni Aversa.

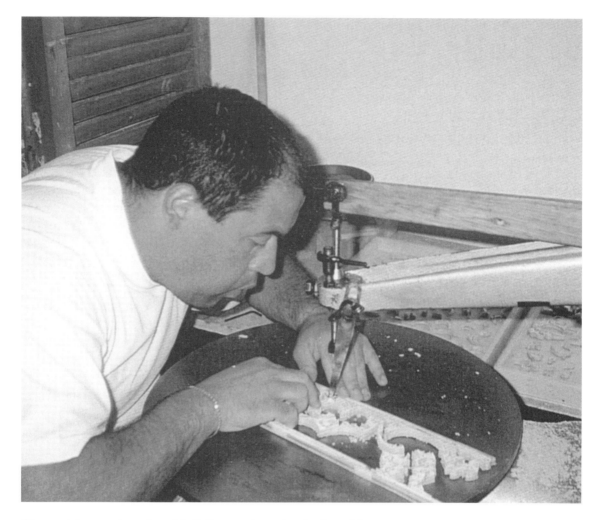

Giovanni Aversa at work on his Italian-made customized machine.

Paul Budd's artistic talents express themselves in many ways, including the creation of complex designs for his special puzzles produced on a Diamond scroll-saw. An ingenious, some might say fiendish, capacity to conjure extreme frustration in even the most experienced 'puzzlers' is evidenced by his layered, three-dimensional, conundrums.

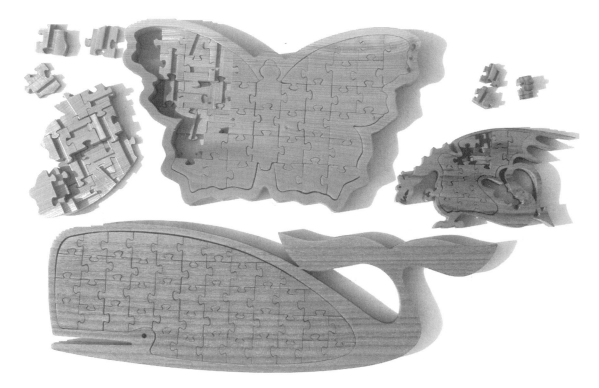

Unusual puzzles designed and created by Paul Budd.

The butterfly, made from yew, is one of Paul Budd's more complex creations; it is approximately 16mm (⅝in) thick in three layers.

An unusual subject for intarsia is the enlargement, to about 600 × 500mm (24 × 20in) of a British postage stamp. Experienced amateur woodworker, though a relative newcomer to intarsia, is Dr Aubrey Brown MBE, winner of many national awards with his Hegner scroll-saw.

(*Left*) Dr Aubrey Brown MBE used intarsia to enlarge a postage stamp.

(*Below*) Appearing here with his 'Hidden Forest' panel, an example from the designs of Judy Gale Roberts and Jerry Boober, Aubrey is holding the Gold Award he won in the National Woodworker Competition.

Stuart King has become a national figure at exhibitions and craft fairs, demonstrating his skills as a traditional craftsman. He also lectures on country crafts and the making of furniture, full size and miniature. Here he is seen operating his 'donkey' (*see* Chapter 1).

Here is a rare example of Stuart King's work, in what should correctly be called encrusting, because after cutting its outline, the motif, cut from sycamore, is laid onto a rosewood base. Commissioned in 1979 by the author's wife, Tricia, from a line drawing in his guitar tutor, *The Complete Guitar Player*.

Stuart King, here seen operating his 'donkey'.

An illustration of how, even with a coarse-grained wood such as ash, with experience and care extremely fine work may be achieved.

The author has researched and made many early instruments on which he performs and lectures. Shown here is a Renaissance lute, based on an original by Hans Frei.

Ornamenting the soundboard is the rose, designed and made by the maker. It is sawn, then carved to give the impression of being woven from the wood of the soundboard. The rear panel of the peg-box is decorated with a related motif and the fingerboard is inlaid with a decorative panel. Woods used include: bird's eye maple, holly, rosewood and spruce.

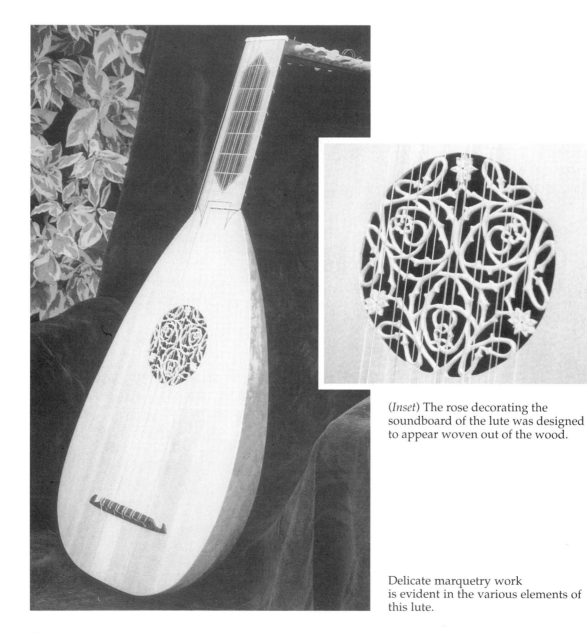

(*Inset*) The rose decorating the soundboard of the lute was designed to appear woven out of the wood.

Delicate marquetry work is evident in the various elements of this lute.

(*Right*) The lute's peg box inlaid with a motif related to the rose pattern.

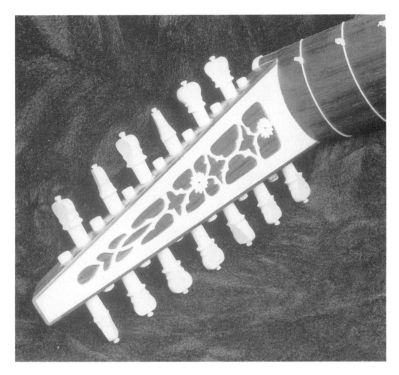

(*Below*) Few would expect to recognize the Organistrum, a mediaeval hurdy-gurdy, the result of many years of research into 12th-century musical instruments. This was made from the author's studies in many parts of Europe. Many woodworking techniques are involved with its creation: unusual joints, bending, turning, carving and, of course, scrollsawing.

10 Projects

HOUSE NUMBER PLATE

Lesson to learn: Sawing in a straight line, with table set horizontally or at an angle.

Material recommended: Exterior grade plywood, solid hardwood or MDF between 6mm (¼in) and 12mm (½in).

Blade range: Fixed speed: 10 to 12 t.p.i. Variable speed: Up to about 1,000 s.p.m., 10 to 12 t.p.i.

Here is the most straightforward project of them all: a number plate for the house. Rather than a square shape, a parallelogram was used, just to be different. Of course an oval or a circle would do equally, or any other shape if desired.

Material for the plate may be solid wood, MDF or plywood. If the latter is chosen it should be of the exterior grade, to withstand an outdoor environment. Almost any thickness will do, providing that it is sufficient to take the screws used to fix the numbers.

Stage 1

Lay out the numbers, evenly spaced, on the chosen material and arrange them in whatever way is pleasing.

Rule on lines to leave a parallel border around the numbers. Mark the positions for the pilot holes for the screens.

Brass numbers are laid on the plywood board and positioned at a diagonal. A border is drawn to indicate the finished size of the plate.

A pin-ended blade with coarse teeth was used to cut out the plate. The table could be set at an angle to leave a bevelled edge on the sides.

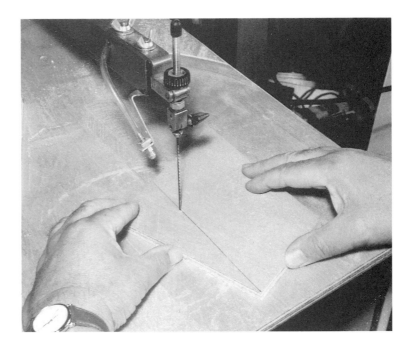

Stage 2

Use a coarse blade and cut along the lines. Make the most of this as an opportunity to practise the skill of line-following. Cut either on the outside or the inside of the line, or even try to divide the line, leaving an equal amount showing on each side of the cut! It won't matter much if there is a slight deviation, since the number plate has not got to fit another component.

It might be an opportunity to try out the facility to tilt the saw table at an angle of, say, 15 degrees, to leave a bevel edge all round. Why not? Remember to make the cuts follow an anti-clockwise direction around the periphery if you are looking at the outer face of the plate if you wish to have the bevel showing.

Stage 3

Drill two holes to accept screws for the fixing of the plate to the wall. With care these may be positioned so that the numbers will cover the screws when in place.

Finish the plate in paint, varnish or whatever suits the location and decor; screw it to the wall and fix the numbers.

Prior to screwing the plate to the wall, the numbers are positioned and screwed on temporarily. Having ascertained their location the numbers were removed and holes inserted at points covered by the numbers.

ROCKING SEAL

Lesson to learn: Cutting curves and navigating sharp corners.

Material recommended: Plywood, solid wood or MDF. From 12mm (½in) to 25mm (1in)

Blade range: Fixed speed: 12 to 15 t.p.i.
Variable speed: About 1200 s.p.m., 12 t.p.i.

This jolly chap is an ideal threshold project. It may be made in MDF, plywood or solid timber.

Stage 1

Prepare a template from the pattern shown in Fig. 21. If a plastic material, card or thin ply is used, it may be used several times, rather than a paper template glued on to the material.

Stage 2

Choose a piece of material of a size close to that of the seal, to reduce waste and the

Fig. 21 Rocking seal pattern. 10mm grid lines.

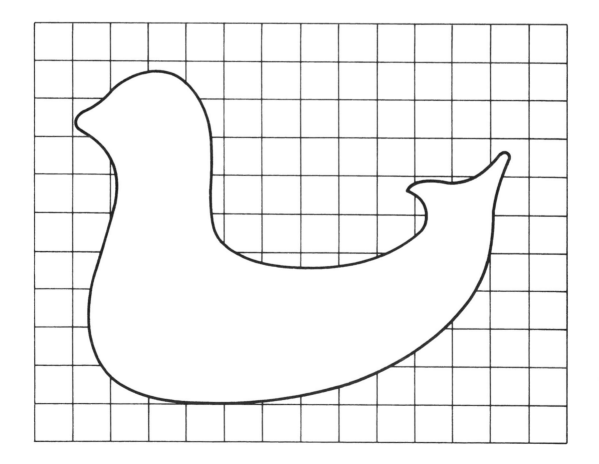

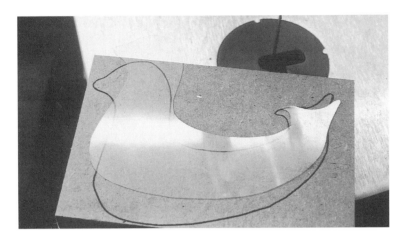

A template prepared from transparent plastic was used to transfer the shape of the seal to the 25mm (1in) blank.

(*Below*) A basic, single-speed, C-framed scrollsaw was used with a pin-ended coarse blade to cut out the seal. A stout line made with a felt-tip pen was easy to follow.

sawing time from the edge of the material to contact with the line of the pattern.

Trace around the template with a sharp, hard pencil or a fine felt-tip pen.

Stage 3

Load the machine with a coarse blade; a pin-ended blade will be fine for this. Commence sawing at the tail and decide for the sake of the practice whether you will follow the line by cutting along the outside edge, the inside edge or by dividing it into

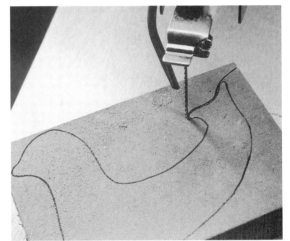

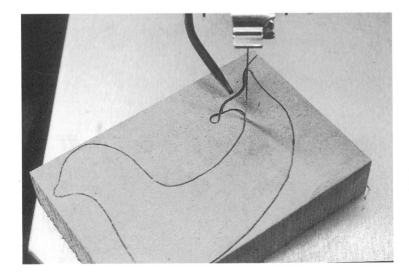

Since the sharp point on the tail is impossible to navigate by following the line continuously, a small loop is cut away from the design into the waste. This allows a return to the line to produce the desired sharp corner.

81

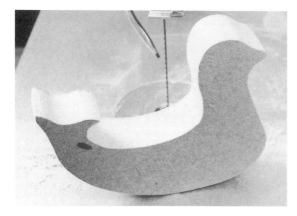

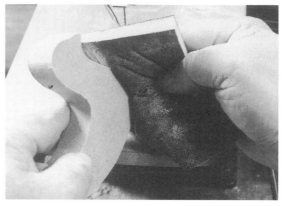

Although the waste broke at the bottom edge, the sawing of the seal was completed in one unbroken line.

The sides of the workpiece were quite smooth from the sawing, despite the relatively coarse blade. The structure of MDF is such that it has a tendency to leave a slightly broken bottom edge; this was removed with a foam-packed abrasive pad.

two. Don't worry if the cut deviates from time to time; there is no critical dimension to be concerned about in this project, but it is good practice for the occasions in the future when accuracy is important.

Notice how the pointed edge of the tail is negotiated, by following a circular path in order to leave a sharp corner. This is quite difficult to achieve with an on-the-spot turn, particularly with a coarse blade.

Continue to follow the line until the seal outline is completed.

Stage 4

Clean up the corners of the seal, if necessary, with fine abrasive paper and paint or varnish as desired.

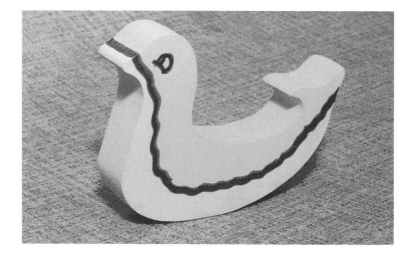

With his new suit and ready for his first outing, the seal should appeal to toddlers as he rocks at the touch of a small hand. In case his little friends attempt to discover how he tastes, remember to use paints approved for nursery use.

ART NOUVEAU MIRROR

Lesson to learn: Navigating smaller radii and sustaining a long curved cut.

Material recommended: Plywood or MDF.

Blade range: Fixed speed: 12 to 15 t.p.i.
Variable speed: up to 1,800 s.p.m., 12 to 20 t.p.i.

A somewhat fancy title for a rather simple mirror, but why not? This is another straightforward project with a useful and decorative function based on a style of the early twentieth century when curves were 'in'. Of course almost any outer shape will do; this happens to have been worked around an oval mirror. A glazier was asked to produce an oval shape a little larger than a hand.

The oval was drawn onto a piece of card and the inner and outer shapes drawn on, to leave a border of glass for gluing.

Use wood or MDF, no more than 12mm (½in), preferably 5mm (³⁄₁₆in).

Stage 1

Acquire an oval mirror to the pattern shown and make a card template as per the pattern. Alternatively, make a paper pattern and stick it onto the material chosen for the frame.

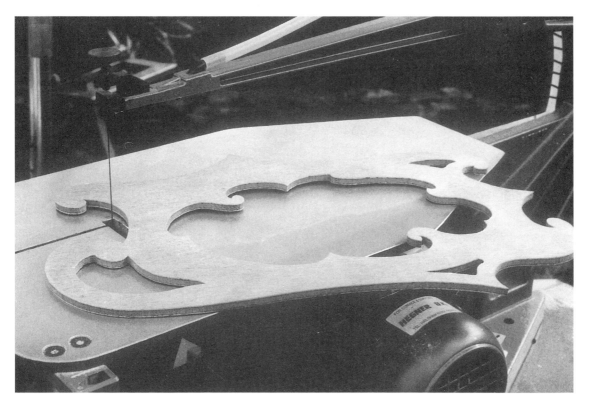

Lying on the table of a parallel arm machine, the completed frame for the Art Nouveau mirror.

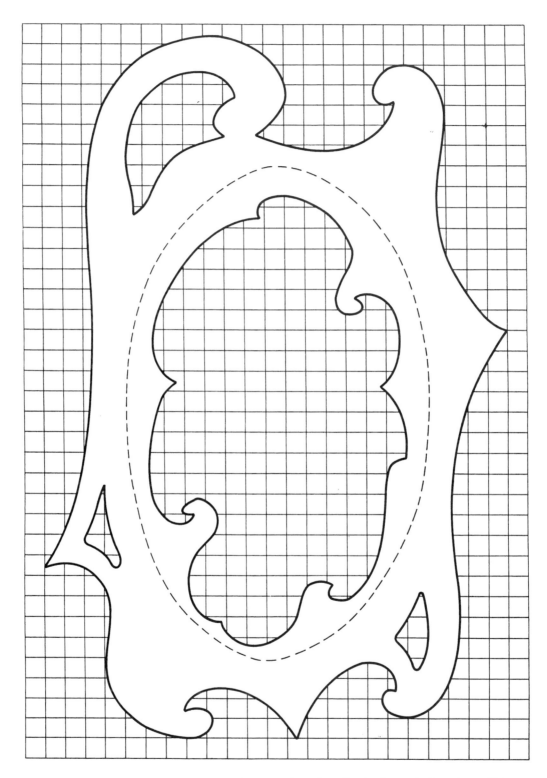

Fig. 22 Pattern for the Art Nouveau mirror. Shown in dotted outline is the oval glass that will be fixed with adhesive.

Fig. 23 Alternative pattern for an Art Nouveau mirror.

Stage 2

Drill access holes for the sawing of the inner portion and the other apertures.

Stage 3

Proceed to cut out the apertures, remembering how we negotiated the sharp corners on the seal. Use the same technique here where necessary to produce those points.

Ready to hang. The oval glass has been glued to the frame.

Stage 4

Cut out the outer shape and smooth off all edges.

Stage 5

The example was finished in pink emulsion with a 'blush' of gold enamel sprayed on from a can.

Stage 6

Epoxy resin was used to fix the glass to the frame.

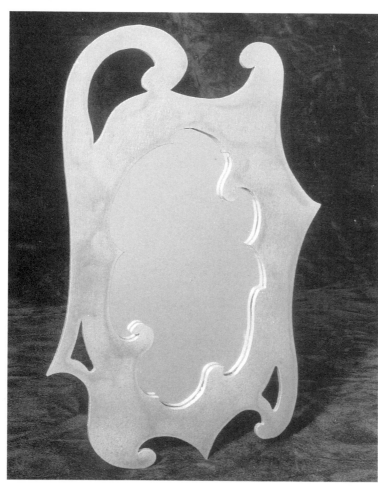

GEMMA'S JIGSAW PUZZLE

Lesson to learn:	Drawing freehand saw-lines and following simple or complex curves.
Material recommended:	Hardwood-faced plywood, or MDF, up to 12mm thick.
Blade range:	Fixed speed: 12 to 15 t.p.i. Variable speed: About 1,000 s.p.m., 15 to 20 t.p.i.

Here is a favourite with any child. If you have no child or grandchild, try to borrow one – they are ideal subjects for this type of project.

Take an enlarged photograph or some other suitable picture that will have some meaning to whoever will be the lucky person to receive it. Photographs work well if copied onto paper by a good quality photocopier.

Use a good quality birch ply for this.

Stage 1

Dilute some PVA white adhesive with 10% water and use it to glue the picture to the wood. Weight it down to prevent bubbling or creasing and leave it for several hours to dry out completely.

Stage 2

When dry, place a piece of card on top of the picture and fix it temporarily with masking tape around the edge.

The photograph selected has been photocopied and stuck to the MDF backing. A piece of card will cover the picture; this will be used to mark the saw lines.

Masking tape is used to fix the card temporarily to the mounted picture.

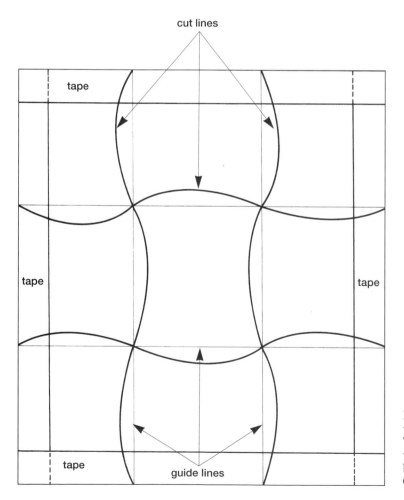

Fig. 24 Development of the wavy jigsaw puzzle saw-lines. This pattern is intended for the very young child (and the beginner scrollsawyer!). Compare with Fig. 25.

Stage 3

Divide up the face of the pack with ruled pencil lines, making nine squares.

Stage 4

Using the straight lines as a guide, draw wavy lines to create the saw cuts for the puzzle pieces. Freehand drawing is adequate for this.

Stage 5

Saw along the wavy lines with a fine blade, 'O' gauge for instance. Two cuts will divide the piece into three pieces.

Having drawn the wavy lines, guided by the straight divisions, the pack is presented for sawing.

(*Below*) Following the wavy lines the pack is cut into three along its length.

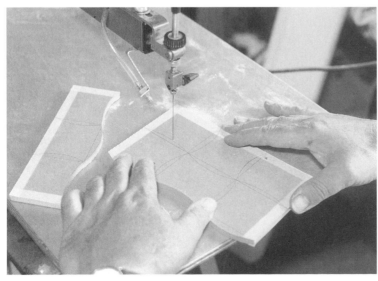

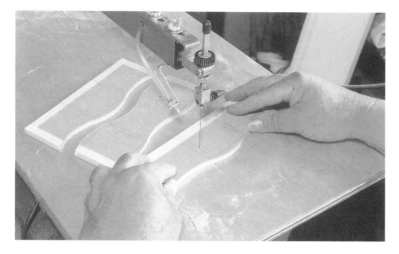

Cross-cutting of the three pieces into nine.

Gemma, preserved for all time with a pretty bouquet and a matching smile.

Stage 6

Saw the three pieces across the remaining wavy lines, making nine pieces.

Stage 7

Remove the tape and card and there is the personalized jigsaw puzzle to delight any child. Maybe their delight would be increased if they saw the whole procedure and maybe even 'helped' to create it?

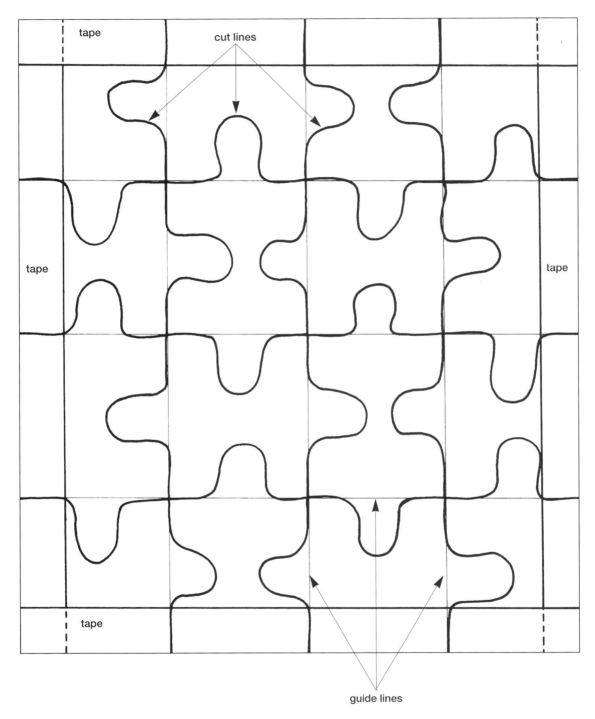

Fig. 25 A more demanding jigsaw pattern, developed from a straight line grid, drawn freehand.

GOTHIC MIRROR

Lesson to learn: Sawing at a specific angle to produce a triangulated section.

Material recommended: Multi-ply veneered in hardwood, or MDF, 6mm (¼in) thick.

Blade range: Fixed speed: 12 to 15 t.p.i.
Variable speed: 750 s.p.m., 13 to 20 t.p.i.

Here is a project in more intricate aperture-cutting with the table tilted to cut the internal edges at a bevel. The design is based on shapes found in ecclesiastical windows and screens.

The apertures are more than just holes with fancy shapes, because the effect is enhanced by the aperture walls being cut at an angle to the face.

Fig 26 Gothic mirror pattern. The mirror in section view shows the bevelled edges of the sawn sides and how they form triangles in narrow portions

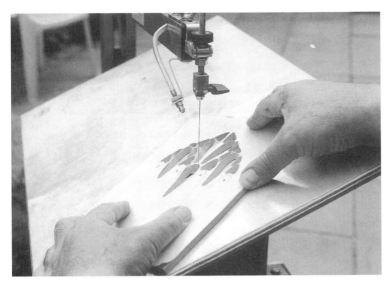

Sawing at an angle with the table set down at the left by about 15 degrees, to cut the internal sides of the apertures.

(*Below*) The bevelled edges of the internal tracery give a more delicate look to the mirror, and the stained varnish enhances its appearance.

Stage 1

Produce a copy of the given pattern, stick it onto a piece of ply or MDF and drill an access hole in each aperture.

Stage 2

Set the saw table at, say, 15 degrees and cut out the apertures, following the lines in an anti-clockwise direction.

Stage 3

Remove any burrs left by the saw and finish the surface as desired. In the example, a combined varnish-stain was used.

Stage 4

Apply an epoxy resin adhesive sparingly to the rear face of the frame and press it under gentle pressure against the glass, until set.

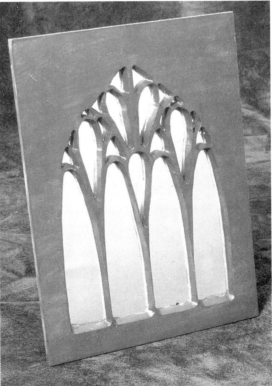

BOOKENDS

Lesson to learn: Extensive pierced work in relatively thick material.

Material recommended: MDF up to 20mm (¾in).

Blade range: Fixed speed: 12 to 15 t.p.i.
Variable speed: 500 to 750 s.p.m., 12 to 18 t.p.i.

Another chance to try some aperture-cutting of a decorative kind with a useful function. This time the material is thicker, up to say 25mm (1in); solid wood, ply or MDF may be used.

Stage 1

Cut a template from card or plastic using the given pattern as a guide, or design your own.

All the apertures are pierced, ready for the sawing of the waste voids.

Note the spiral approach to a circular line, to avoid an abrupt entry that could leave a bump.

Stage 2

Choose a piece of material, preferably with a right-angle corner already prepared, and trace an outline on it from the template. Alternatively, it is possible to stick together two pieces of, say, 12mm (½in), and cut out both pieces simultaneously. Double-sided tape is fine for this job.

Stage 3

Drill holes for blade access in each aperture. It is best to drill them near corners to help negotiate the blade.

Fig. 27 Book-end pattern. Two are needed thus, but they may be cut simultaneously.

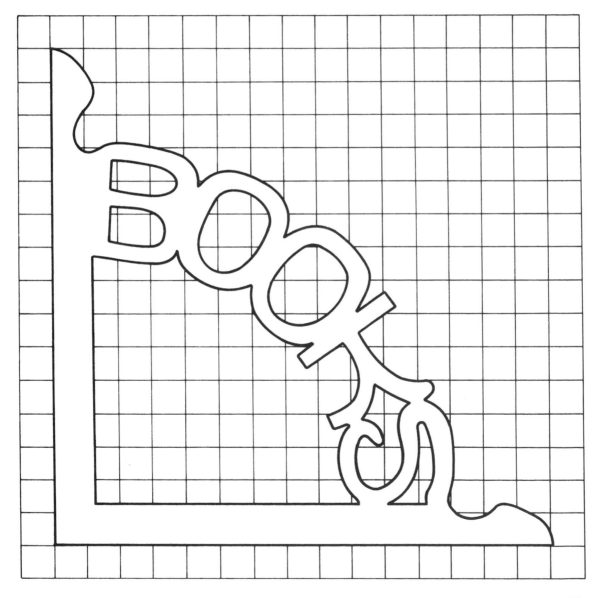

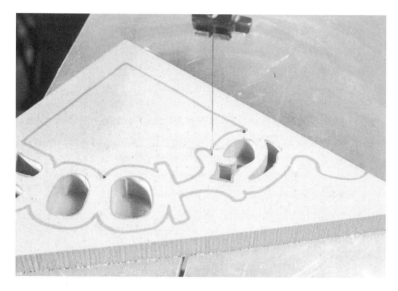

To navigate a sharp corner, the workpiece has been drawn back slightly, for the blade to re-enter at a different angle before continuing.

Fig. 28 Position of screws used to attach the brackets to the books to make up the book-ends. Length of screws and their location must be judged carefully, and correct pilot holes must be drilled to prevent splitting of the material (*below*).

Stage 4

Cut out all the apertures leaving the larger one till last.

Stage 5

Saw the outer shape and trim off all burrs.

Stage 6

Repeat for the second piece. (Unless at Stage 2 it was decided to cut two together, in which case, divide the two pieces.)

Stage 7

Paint or varnish as required.

Stage 8

Choose four books of sufficient size to permit the brackets to sit within the covers.

Assemble the books and brackets, marking the covers with a pencil to show where the brackets touch. Note which brackets and books are associated.

Brackets are more or less identical and painted with contrasting outlines.

Assembly of the books and brackets, using countersunk screws.

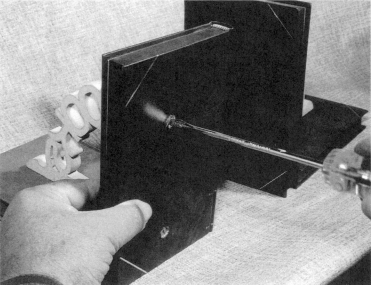

Stage 9

Mark centres for the screw holes on the book covers and drill through from the side touching the bracket. Countersink from the other side to accept the fixing screws. Screw size will depend on thickness of book and bracket. Remember to keep length of screw to less than the combined thicknesses.

Stage 10

Assemble the brackets and books again as previously associated and mark the brackets through the screw-holes in the books to indicate the positions of the screws.

Stage 11

Choose a drill of a diameter equivalent to the core size of the screw and of sufficient depth to pilot the screw into the bracket without splitting it. Drill the four holes in each bracket.

Stage 12

Mount the brackets on the books and there are the book ends, ready for work.

An attractive feature for a library; ready to house those special editions.

ORNAMENTAL CANDLE SCONCE

Lesson to learn: Cutting intricate curves and accurate mostise and tenon joints. Cutting circular components with table tilted.

Material recommended: Multi-ply or MDF about 6mm (¼in) thick.

Blade range: Fixed speed: 14 to 18 t.p.i. Variable speed: 350 to 500 s.p.m., 14 to 20 t.p.i.

Intended primarily as an ornament, this candle sconce can be made in either plywood or MDF; both were used in the given example. Best if the candle-holders are fitted with metal inserts – small paint-pot lids, for instance – as a safeguard against fire.

In the example described, 5mm plywood was used for the bracket and the candle holders cut from 25mm MDF.

Stage 1

It is best to draw the component parts onto the material from templates traced from the patterns illustrated herein. It is possible to cut them from paper, glue them onto the material and cut them out directly. Two minor hazards pertain to this method, one being the possible distortion of the paper due to contact with the glue and the other is the problem of removing the paper pattern after cutting out the template. If low-tack adhesive is used, fine, but otherwise best to use the following method, which also preserves the template for further use.

The technique of 'mirroring' is used to prepare two of the components, namely the wall-plate (a) and the shelf (b). A useful little trick that might have other applications, it is done as follows.

1. Trace the outline of the bracket components, a, b and c, on transparent paper, or make a copy using carbon paper. If

Patterns are prepared and traced onto the plywood.

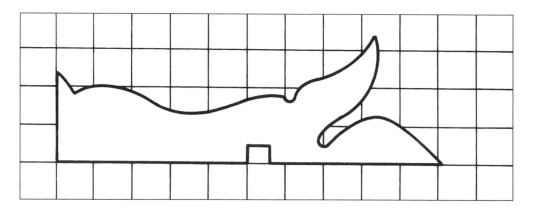

(*Above*) Fig. 29 Quarter-pattern for the wall-plate (a); *see* text on how it is used.

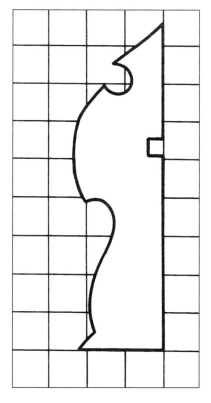

(*Left*) Fig. 30 Platform (b), also shown as a quarter-pattern.

Fig. 31 This holder is designed to take a standard domestic-sized candle. Other sizes could be catered for if need be.

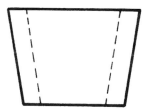

you have access to a photocopier, even better. Carefully cut out the tracings.

2. Outlines a and b represent quarters of their respective components and these are first cut out of the paper on which they were traced.

3. Take a piece of stiff card or plastic sheet, thin enough to cut with scissors, and a pencil.

4. Draw a line, with a ruler, about the length of the component and divide it in its centre with another line drawn at

right angles corresponding to the approximate width of the component.

5. Place one of the cut-out tracings on the card with its long straight edge in line with the longest drawn line, bringing the short edge to coincide with the cross-line.
6. Draw around the periphery.
7. Turn the tracing over, lining up the long edge with the long line again to make a mirror-image with the previously drawn pattern.
8. Draw around the periphery.
9. By turning the tracing over twice more, to mirror those already drawn in similar fashion, it is a straightforward process to complete the drawing of the complete component.
10. Cut out the template and prepare one similarly for component b.

The template for the serpentine bracket (c), is made straight from the tracing.

Stage 2

Having transferred all the template shapes to the material, (remember, two of the serpentine brackets are needed) proceed to cut them out. Some of the sharp curves and points are tricky and following lines will be easier if cutting is taken at a relatively slow feed with a correspondingly slow stroke rate, if the machine has a variable speed.

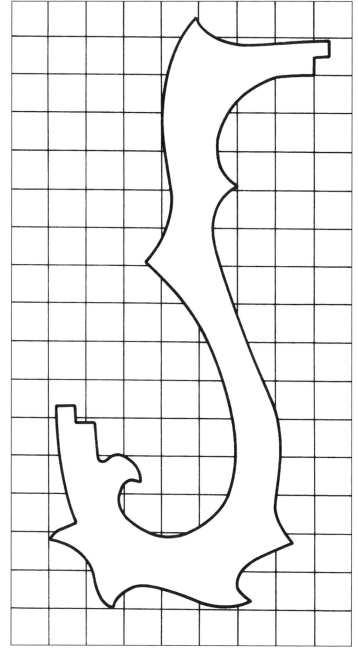

Fig. 32 Bracket pattern (c) shown full size; two of these are needed for the candle sconce.

A basic machine with a coarse blade was used for cutting the bracket components.

Care must be taken to match the size of the mortises (the square holes in the wall plate and the candle-support) with the tenons on the serpentine brackets.

When the components are cut out, it is best to remove any burrs left on the cut edges by cleaning up with a fine abrasive. An abrasive pad with a foam sandwich filling is ideal for this purpose since it follows curves readily.

Assemble the four components temporarily, making any adjustments necessary to fit the mortises and tenons accurately. When all parts are fitting satisfactorily, glue the assembly.

Stage 3

Using a piece of 25mm (1in) MDF, circles are drawn representing the inner and outer diameters of the candle-holders. Drill a centre hole not less than 6mm (¼in) to access the blade. Remember two candle-holders are needed.

Setting the saw table at 10 degrees down on the left (or 100 degrees between the

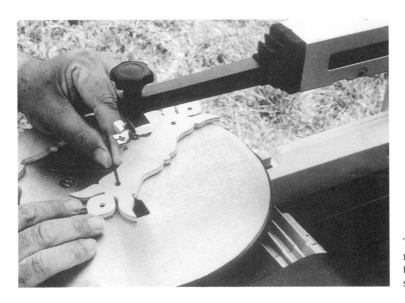

Threading the blade through the mortise holes. These are squared to accept the tenons in the serpentine brackets.

Foam abrasive pads are practical for removing unwanted burrs.

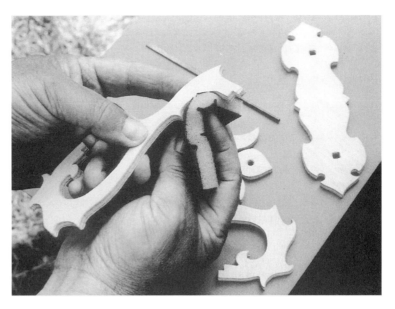

blade and the left-hand side of the table), thread a coarse blade through the hole and attach it to the saw frames.

Working from the centre hole in a spiral gradually approach the diameter of the inner circle and cut out the centre portion. Repeat for the second holder. There should now be two tapered holes in the MDF. Keep the table setting as for the inner diameters and cut out the holders by sawing around the larger of the diameters, approaching in a spiral from the edge. Trim off any burrs on the holders and glue them into position on the sconce.

With the table set down 10 degrees on the left, the candle cups are sawn. Note the spiral entry for the inner part to remove the waste. On the lower side of the block is a large hole; this was the result of a trial run, but the cup was too large.

103

A final check on the assembly prior to gluing.

Finish to suit the decor. A metallic black paint was used in the example, that on second thoughts would have been more effective if matt rather than satin were used.

Remember to fit small metal inserts to hold the candles to prevent fire.

Fig. 33 Assembled components making up the candle sconce.

Black was chosen as a colour to give the impression of wrought iron.

To help find the most effective position, the sconce was fixed to the wall temporarily with Blu-tak. Fine for trial tests, but permanent fixing with this method is not recommended.

BRIAN, THE BRONTOSAURUS

Lesson to learn: Cutting extended unbroken curves, in thick material, with some dimensional accuracy required. Cutting secondary dimension to model a shape.

Material recommended: MDF or plywood, 20 to 25mm (¾–1in) thick.

Blade range: Fixed speed: 11 to 14 t.p.i. Variable speed: 500 to 1,000 s.p.m., 11 to 14 t.p.i.

Brian will entertain children and the not-so-grown-ups with his lumbering, rocking plod down an inclined board. He would have been the length of four cars and twice as heavy!

This project introduces cutting on two planes, meaning the effect is a three dimensional one, like a sculpture. 25mm (1in) MDF is recommended for Brian.

Stage 1

Trace the outline of the body, side elevation, onto a piece of 25mm (1in) thick MDF.

Stage 2

Saw out the body with great care to preserve accuracy. Aim to split the line.

Sawing of the outline is completed except for the slot that accepts the wire connector.

Fig. 34 Two views of the brontosaurus; plan and side elevation. When scaling, use the 10mm grid lines as a guide, taking care that the positions of the legs are correctly related.

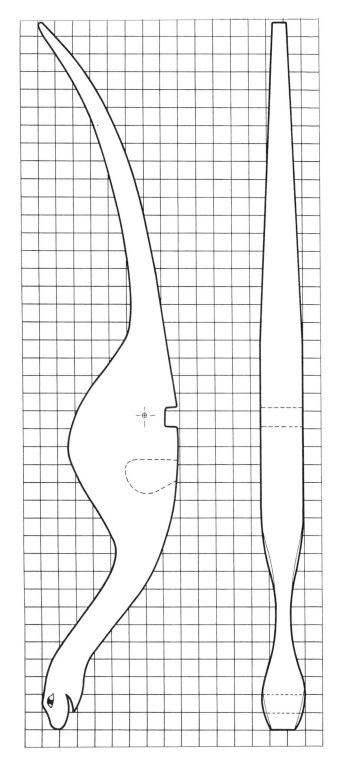

A diagonal cut is made into the corner first, to help clear the waste and to create a clean sharp corner.

Accuracy of size and position is required for this slot to ensure correct movement of the rear legs.

Stage 3

Draw the outline of the plan view on the top of the body.

Stage 4

Cut out the waste from the sides of the body to produce the form of the head, neck and tail. Since the underneath of the body is the base in contact with the table, care must be taken to ensure that the workpiece is stable during the sawing operation. For example, see that, before the head and neck are commenced, the piece is resting firmly on its lower jaw and chest.

Conversely, when sawing the sides of the tail, the piece must be gently rocked as the the cutting proceeds, so that contact is maintained between the piece and the table at the blade insertion. It may sound complicated but in practice it is quite straightforward.

Stage 5

Smooth all edges ready for painting.

Stage 6

Mark out two back legs, side elevation, on 25mm (1in) thick MDF.

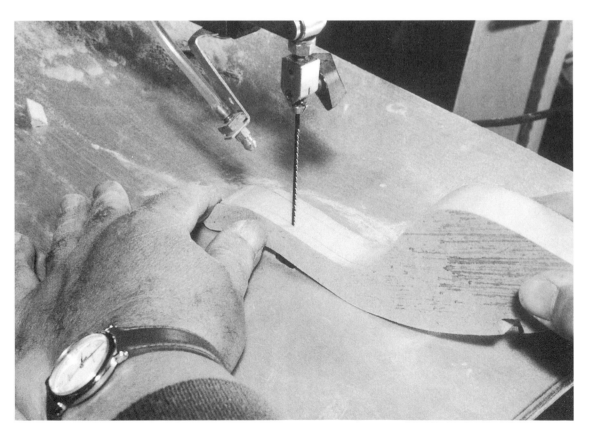

Modelling of the head and neck by removing waste from the sides.

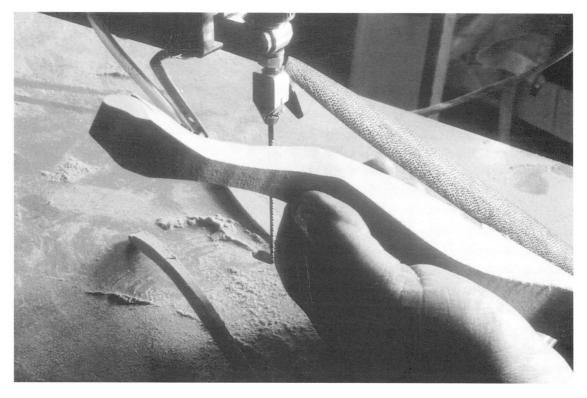

Smoothing out all angular changes of the contours.

Brian is waiting for his legs.

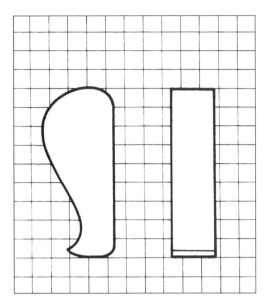

Fig. 35 Front leg, two needed, for the brontosaurus.

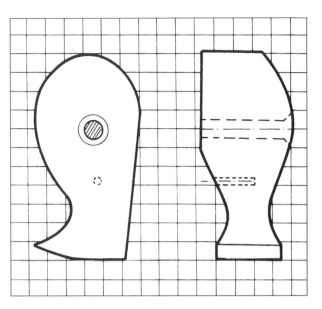

Fig. 36 Rear leg, two needed, for the brontosaurus.

Stage 7

Cut out two back legs.

Stage 8

Acquire two fixing screws to act as pivots for the back legs and a piece of stiff wire, as from a coat hanger. Two washers are needed to place between the back legs and the body to ensure free movement of the parts. Two nails will also be needed to attach the front legs.

Stage 9

Drill the holes for the pivot screws and the connecting rod.

Stage 10

Mark the side-shaping on the back legs.

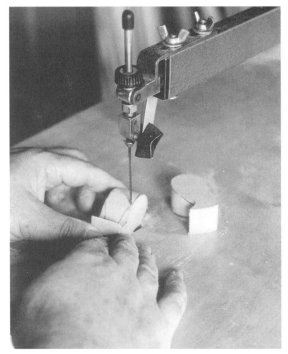

Rear legs are outlined and now being shaped.

111

Stage 11

Cut off the waste from the sides of the back legs.

Stage 12

Trim burrs from all edges ready for painting.

Stage 13

Mark out two front legs on 12mm (½in) MDF.

Stage 14

Cut out the front legs.

Stage 15

Drill two pilot holes for fixing nails.

Stage 16

Trim off burrs ready for painting

Stage 17

Mark the positions of the front legs and glue and nail them onto the body. Check that they are of equal projection below the body so that Brian stands level.

  Leave them to dry.

Stage 18

Mark the positions of the pilot hole for the pivot screws and drill it straight through the body to ensure the alignment of the screws.

Stage 19

Assemble the back legs with the connecting rod, that should push fit into the pilot holes. This makes sure that the legs move as a unit.

Stage 20

Screw the back legs onto the body with the washers between the members.

  The connecting rod should be positioned in the gap beneath the body. This limits the movement of the legs. Check for tightness; this should be sufficient to remove wobble but allow free movement.

Stage 21

Take a piece of ply or hardboard about 1m (3ft) long and rest it on a temporary support. By trial and error, move the support to establish at which angle the board permits the jogging of Brian down the slope. Just a light touch on his tail should send him gently lolloping down, all on his own.

Stage 22

If all is well, disassemble the back legs and paint the dinosaur. Reassemble when dry.

Stage 23

Check the slope angle once more, correcting if necessary, then once it is correctly established, make a permanent run for Brian so that he may be exercised regularly.

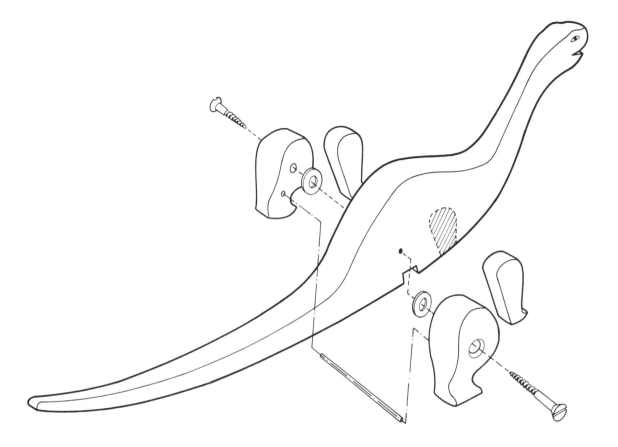

Fig. 37 Exploded view of brontosaurus assembly, showing all components.

Brian is now ready for his downhill romp!

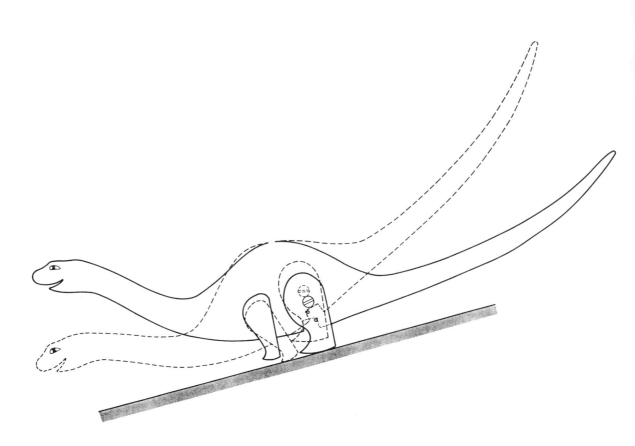

Fig. 38 With the correctly inclined slope, Brian will rock from front foot to back galumphing his way in true brontosaurus fashion.

ETRUSCAN CHARIOT

Lesson to learn: Three-dimensional modelling, precise and intricate sawing.

Material recommended: Solid hardwood, mahogany, box, sycamore, maple, cherry, etc.

Blade range: Fixed speed: 15 to 25 t.p.i, for the thinner sections, 12 to 15 t.p.i. for thicker ones.
Variable speed: 250 to 350 s.p.m., 12 to 15 t.p.i.

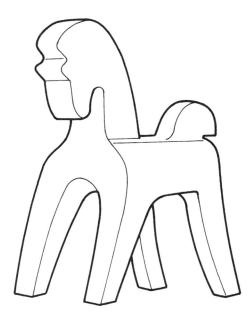

Fig. 39 Etruscan horse (1).

An unusual subject for a scrollsaw, being in effect, a three-dimensional carving!

Inspired by, rather than a copy of, a bronze statuette of a pair of horses pulling a chariot, seen in an art gallery in Florence.

Provided that the sequence of cuts is followed, it is an uncomplicated affair, with an important proviso: because the sawing of the first plane creates a profile, when it is turned over and through 90 degrees for the second cutting, it is not possible to use a hold-down. In fact no hold-down was used for any of the work on this project. A fine opportunity to master the craft of scroll-sawing using unsupported hands.

Making the Horses

Stage 1

Prepare two blocks of the required dimensions with reference to the drawings. Best to work on one horse at a time. Note the horses are slightly different in pose.

Stage 2

Copy the outline of the side elevation of the horse onto the corresponding side of the block.

Fig. 40 Etruscan horse (2).

115

Fig. 41 Three views of the
Etruscan horse (1).

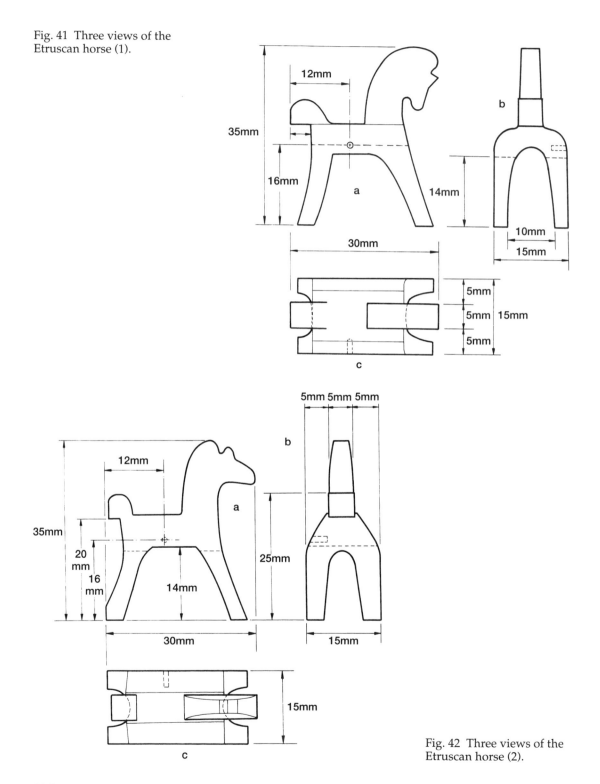

Fig. 42 Three views of the
Etruscan horse (2).

Stage 3

Cut out the waste from the side. In the example shown, the holes for the shaft connection were drilled into the horses after the sawing was completed, but it is theoretically best to drill them now.

Stage 4

Utilize an ancillary 'table'; in the illustration a piece of scrap three-ply was used. The saw blade was entered to a point about half-way through its width. This ensures full support to the workpiece, that otherwise would have been insecure over the aperture in the standard table insert.

Stage 5

Stand the horse on its tail and back legs and draw the outline of the end view on the opposite side. This is like looking at the horse full face – in the mouth, if you choose!

Stage 6

Cut away the waste from the head, neck and shoulders. The outer faces of the legs need no sawing, since they are flat-sided and of the correct size from the block

(*Above*) The side elevation of one horse shape has been drawn and sawn. Here the pieces have been reassembled.

Using a piece of scrap material as an ancillary 'table,' the horse is sitting on its tail and back legs as the waste is sawn from the sides of the head and between the legs.

117

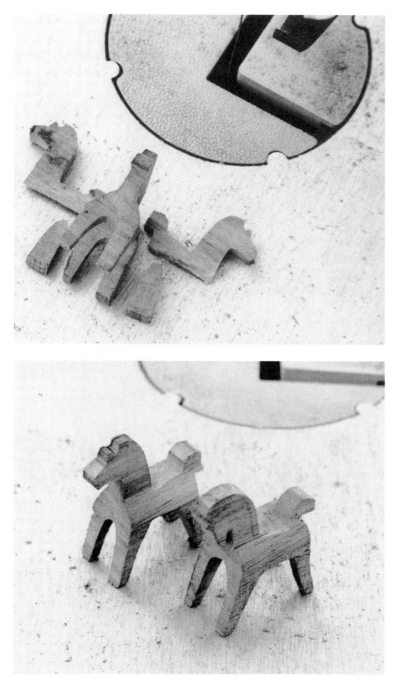

Waste has been cut away from the horse and it is finished, as far as sawing is concerned.

A matched team, ready to receive the chariot.

width. Remove the waste from between the legs too. Since the horse is 'sitting' as it were, gazing up to the sky, it follows that the internal profiles of front and rear legs are shaped simultaneously. During this tricky part of the process, the downwards pressure must be applied by gripping the sides of the workpiece, as the saw is steered around the line. Just another knack to develop…

Apart from minor cleaning up to remove unwanted burrs, the first horse is finished. When standing on its feet, it will be seen that the plan view, looking from above, has been developed automatically from the

Fig. 43 Three views of the Etruscan chariot.

correct sawing of the other two views. If not, something has gone drastically wrong.

If all is well with the first horse, make the second by repeating stages 1 to 6.

The Chariot

Stage 7

Select a suitable piece of wood for the chariot and prepare the width and depth, leaving the length oversize for ease of handling during the first stages of sawing.

Stage 8

Draw at one end of the side of the block, the profile of the chariot depicted in the side elevation of the drawing.

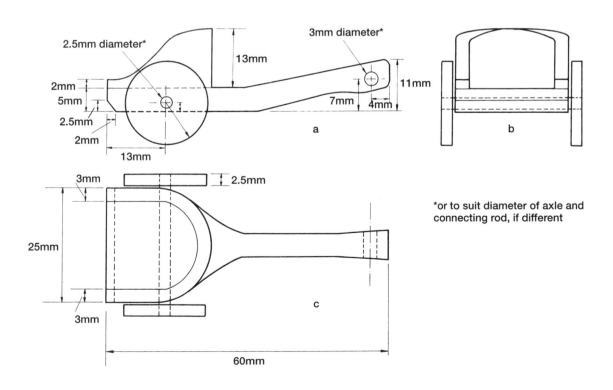

*or to suit diameter of axle and connecting rod, if different

Side elevation of the chariot body is like an elongated letter 'S'. Take care to avoid bumps with the entry and exit cutting. A longer length of blank is used to enable ease of manipulation during the sawing. This will be removed at the last stage of the body sawing.

The inner waste is cut out from the plan view of the chariot body.

Following the outer curve of the chariot body.

Stage 9

Cut out the side view of the chariot body. Do not separate the body from the block at this stage.

Stage 10

Mark out the plan view on the, now curved, top of the workpiece. Effectively this is represented by two parallel lines following the curve of the chariot floor. When sawn from the block it will combine with the previously cut outer edge to form the shaped body.

All three parts of the workpiece, with the inner waste and the body both sawn out.

Stage 11

Cut out the inner curve followed by the outer curve. This should release the upper frame of the chariot body that may be set aside temporarily.

Stage 12

Prepare a block of suitable dimensions for the chassis and shaft. These are combined in one piece and for convenience will be referred to as 'the base'.

Stage 13

Mark on the block the side elevation of the base.

Stage 14

Drill the two holes through the block positioned as shown. Make sure the holes are drilled at right angles through the block.

Use a drill bit of appropriate diameter to accept the cock-tail stick 'axle' with freedom to revolve, but not sloppily.

Stage 15

Saw the waste from the base and, if necessary, level the surface that is to receive the chariot body to ensure a good fit.

Stage 16

Glue the chariot body onto the base and, when the glue is set, mark out the plan outline showing the shaft as part of the base.

Stage 17

Cut away the waste from the body and shaft unit. No particular difficulties should be found here, although care must be taken when cutting the shaft section, because it is raised at an incline, since the base under the body is kept flat on the

Outline of the side elevation is marked and holes have been drilled for the shaft and axle.

Waste removed from the base side elevation.

Having glued the body to the chassis, the shaft is cut and the excess trimmed away from the base to match the body shape.

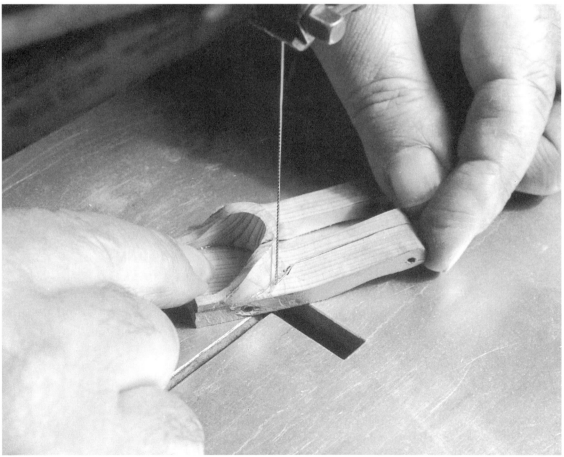

table. The body should act as a guide when trimming away the base. Try to follow this without damaging the sides of the body.

Stage 18

Trim off any excess base material from its edges to bring them flush with the body sides.

Stage 19

Take a piece of 12mm (½in) dowel and slice off two pieces for the wheels. If the dowel is rotated during the sawing it is easy to keep the thickness uniform. Trim off any burrs.

Stage 20

Cut the axle and shaft-connection to length and assemble the seven pieces, adjusting if necessary.

Stage 21

A rub over with an oil varnish should be sufficient to seal and enhance the grain, after which the parts may be reassembled and glued. If the holes in the wheels and horses are drilled to give a tight fit, no glue is necessary. Otherwise, put a spot of glue on the ends of the sticks before assembly, leaving the shaft and base free to move.

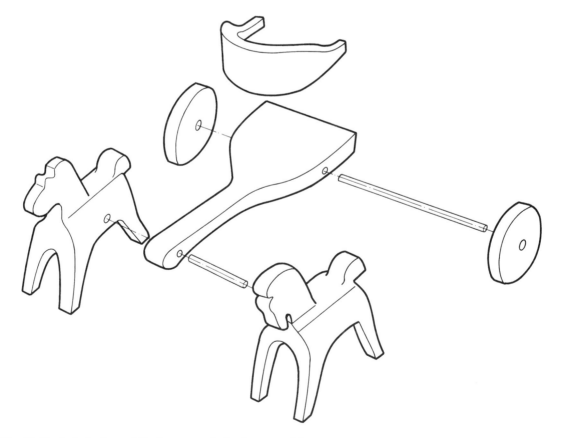

Fig. 44 Exploded view of the horses and chariot assembly.

All components ready for assembly. Light oil varnish is applied to enhance the grain.

Ready for the race!

HUSHABYE MOUNTAIN

Lesson to learn:	Although the piece may be made without strict observation of line, try to use it as a test to navigate the patterns. The lines are long and tortuous, with hairpins and sharp corners.
Material recommended:	MDF or hard-veneered plywood, of about 6mm(¼in) thickness.
Blade range:	Fixed speed: 13 to 15 t.p.i. Variable speed: 200 to 500 s.p.m., 14 to 20 t.p.i

Few would doubt that a child's night-light should be soothing and friendly rather than

spooky. With its contours and layers this gentle light brings to life the little town on the hill suggesting the warmth of bedtime and security of happy homes. During the day it is a colourful ornament.

Vertical panels are made from 4mm (³⁄₁₆in) three-ply, connected at the base with 12mm (½in) MDF. A lamp-holder with a low wattage bulb is needed, plus cable and plug for connection to a power supply; and some lead-free paint and adhesive.

Stage 1

The lamp-holder will be fixed to the base between the two rear panels. In order to reduce the gap between the two panels to a minimum and to establish what that measurement should be, first it will be

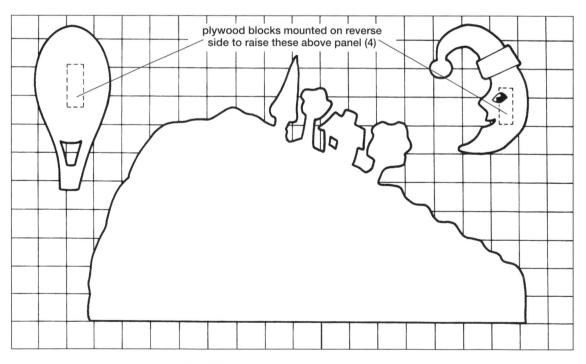

plywood blocks mounted on reverse side to raise these above panel (4)

Fig. 45 Patterns for front panel (1) of Hushabye Mountain, including the moon and the balloon. The latter two will be fixed to the rear panel.

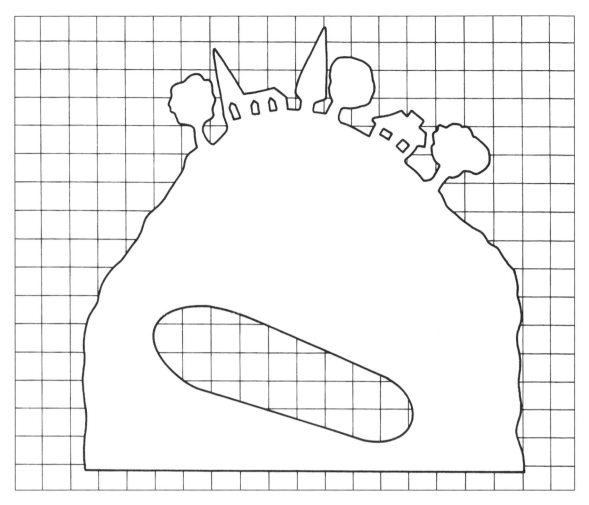

Fig. 46 Front inner panel (2) with aperture for reflected light.

necessary to reduce the width of the lamp-holder base.

A line is scribed either side of and close to the central lamp socket indicating the lines to be sawn.

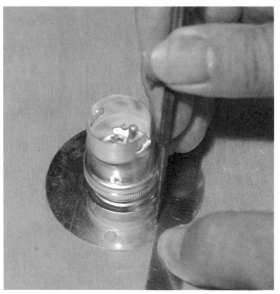

Scribing the lines close to the central socket on the base of the lamp-holder.

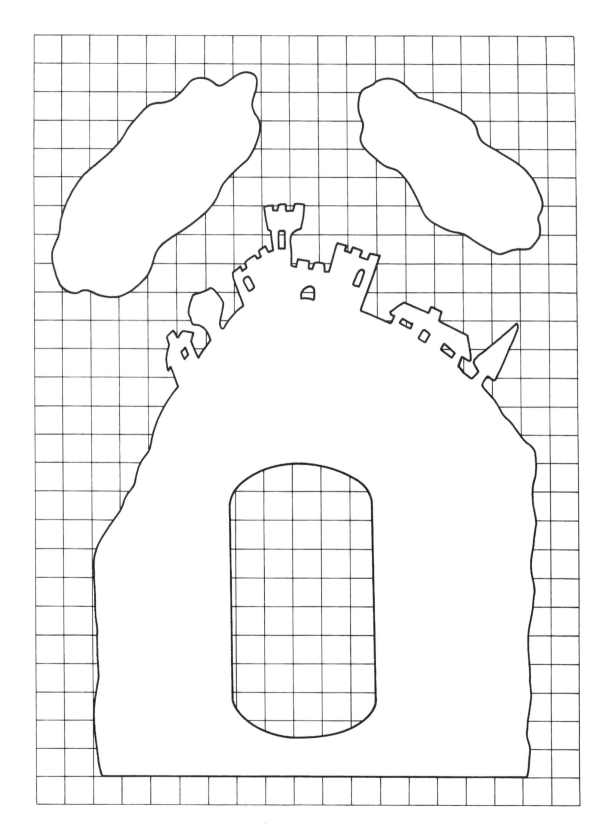

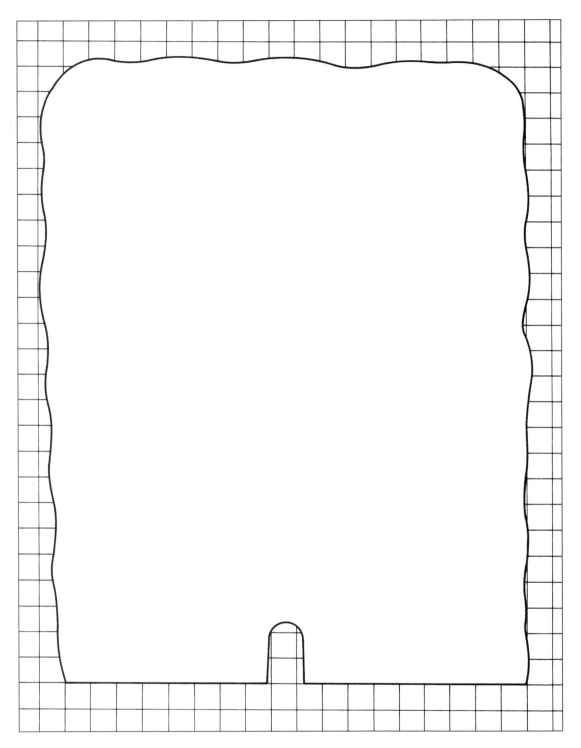

(*Left*) Fig. 47 Rear inner panel (3) of Hushabye Mountain. Both clouds are also detailed here.

(*Above*) Fig. 48 Rear panel (4), with gap at bottom edge for cable access.

(*Right*) Sawing off the waste from the lamp-holder using a fine metal cutting blade.

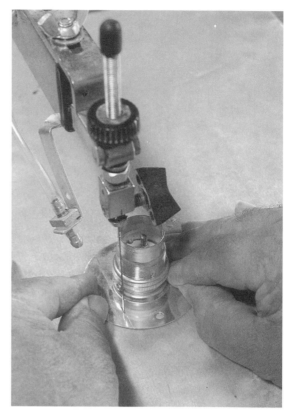

Stage 2

Using a medium-fine metal cutting blade, the waste is cut away from the lamp base. Due to the shape of the lamp-holder , it is almost impossible to use any kind of hold-down effectively, so a constant strong grip is necessary to prevent lifting during the operation.

Raw edges are abraded to remove any sign of sharpness and the lamp-holder is set aside for the moment.

Stage 3

I traced the outlines of all four panels with felt-tipped pen on paper and glued it to individual pieces of plywood to facilitate ease of handling.

Waste has been removed and edges deburred from the base.

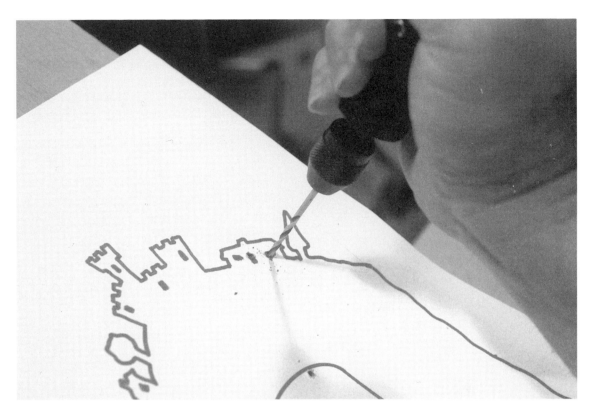

Using a flexible drive fitted to the power take-off on the machine, the access holes are drilled in all four panels.

Stage 4

Holes for the apertures are drilled; I used a drill-bit of about the width of the windows depicted on the patterns. For this, the flexible drive attached to the power take-off was ideal, it being easy to pinpoint the hole positions.

Stage 5

Remember to remove the metal cutting blade used for cutting the lamp-holder and replace it with a moderately fine one intended for wood.

All holes are cut out, including windows, doors and the larger ones that act as light-ways between the panels.

Stage 6

A test of the operator's skills in sharp corner negotiation follows, as the outlines are sawn on all four panels, including those essential light-ways. Even if the design is not geometrically critical, nor the measurements needful of great accuracy, there remains the requirement to be faithful to the outline for the sake of proportion, not to mention self-satisfaction!

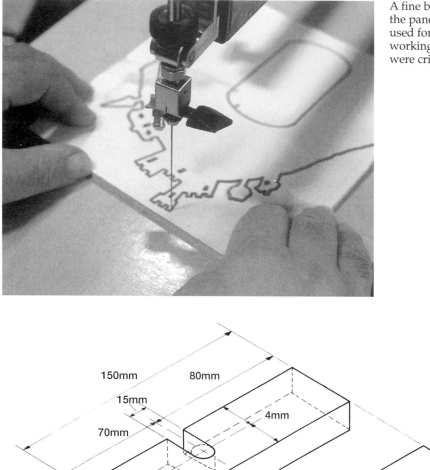

A fine blade is used to cut out all the panels. Red felt-tip pen was used for the outline for ease of working since no measurements were critical.

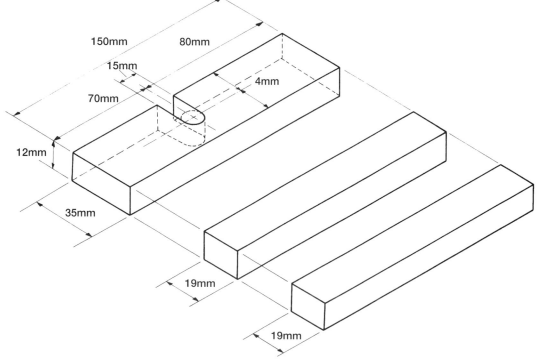

Fig. 49 Detail of the three bases. The one between the rearmost panels must be adequate in width to receive the particular lamp base.

The wooden components are finished and painted.

Stage 7

Make the bases according to the widths given, bearing in mind that the width of the base between the two rear panels is dictated by the particular lamp-holder being used. The gap for the cable is also cut during this operation.

Stage 8

Paint all nine pieces with lead-free paint. The bases and back faces of the panels are painted white to help reflect the light.

Stage 9

Connect the cable to the lamp-holder and fix it to the base with screws.

Stage 10

Fast epoxy adhesive was used in all cases. If there is a shortage of appropriate clamps, panel pins may be used as an alternative to hold pieces during the glue-setting periods.

The gluing sequence is important, as follows:

Fixing of the lamp-holder to make sure the cable runs clear through the gap in the rear base.

(*Below*) Clouds are glued to the sky corners of the rear panel. Small blocks are glued to the backs of the balloon and the moon, since these stand out from the panel.

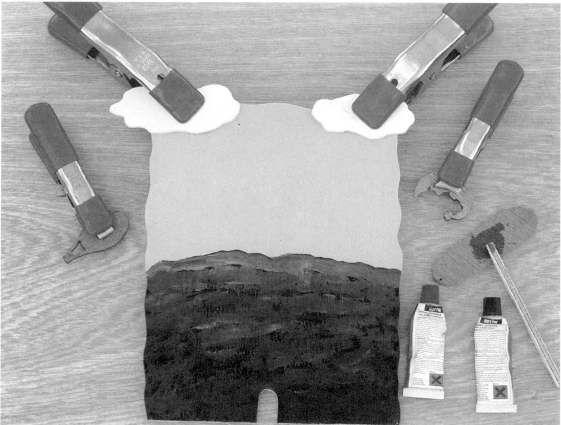

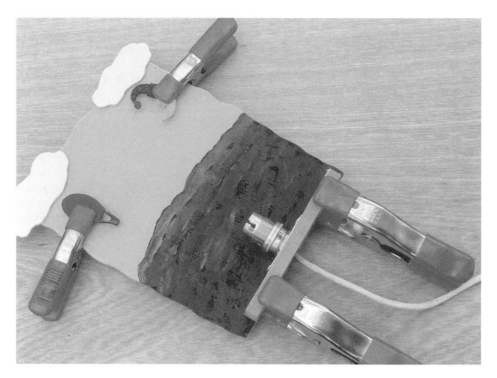

(*Above*) All three parts, balloon, moon and base with the lamp-holder are glued.

(*Below*) Remaining bases are glued, one between the two foremost panels.

1. Clouds to top corners of the sky on the rear panel.
2. Balloon, moon and base to the painted face of rear panel. Note: base and panel must be assembled with the gaps meeting, to permit cable access from the rear.
3. Base to rear inner panel and base between front panels.

There should now be three sub-assemblies: rear panel with lamp-holder, rear inner panel with base and two front panels connected with a shared base.

(*Right*) E Z Hold clamps were used for the final assembly, but alternatively, weights might be improvised.

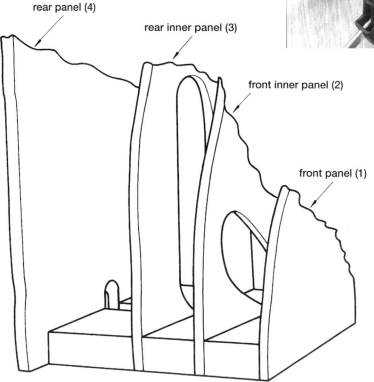

rear panel (4)

rear inner panel (3)

front inner panel (2)

front panel (1)

Fig. 50 Assembly of the panels and bases, showing the alignment of the apertures in the inner panels to convey the reflected light from the lamp. Note, the lamp is fitted before assembling the bases and panels.

Stage 11

All three panel sets are now glued together using clamps. The assembly may be laid flat and weighted in the absence of clamps. Care must be taken to see that the bases are all aligned to create a flat base.

Stage 12

Remove the completed light assembly from the clamps.

Wait for nightfall, plug in, switch on and wait for the 'oohs' and 'ahs' from the children.

The completed Hushabye Mountain.

Appendix

Scrollsaws – Technical specifications

Make	Model	C-frame or Parallel arm	Throat capacity in/mm	Stroke depth (mm)	Strokes per minute	Max depth of cut in/mm	Table tilt L–R	Speed control type	Motor power watts	Dust ext. port	Dust blower	Weight Kg
Diamond	Light 16	P	16.5/410	25	0–1,600	3/75	45–25	Variable	375	No	Yes	N/A
Diamond	AF-19VS	P	20/510	30	0–1,400	4/100	45–0	Variable	375	No	Yes	17
Diamond	AF-24VS	P	25/635	30	0–1,400	4/100	45–0	Variable	375	No	Yes	20
Draper	FS16A	P	16/400	19	1,450	2/50	45–0	None	93	Yes	Yes	20/23
Draper	FS325A	P	13/325	12	1,335	2/50	45–0	None	93	Yes	Yes	12/13
Draper	FS400A	P	16/400	19	1,450	2/50	45–0	None	93	Yes	Yes	14/15.5
Draper	FS500E	P	20/508	22	400–1,800	2/50	45–0	Variable	125	Yes	Yes	24.5/28
Dremel	1371	C	13/330	8	1,350	2/50	45–0	None	110	Yes	No	14
Dremel	1695	P	16/406	18	200–2,000	2/50	45–0	Variable	110	Yes	Yes	18.2
Hegner	Multicut 1	P	14	12	1,700	2/50	45–0	None *	80	Yes	Yes	14
Hegner	Multicut 2S	P	18	6 or 15	1,700	2.625/67	45–15	None *	100	Yes	Yes	21
Hegner	Multicut SE	P	18	6 or 15	400–1,700	2.625/67	45–15	Variable	100	Yes	Yes	23
Hegner	Multicut 3	P	25	10 or 20	400–1,700	2.375/60	45–15	None *	100	Yes	Yes	30
Hegner	Polycut	P	19.5	14 or 24	700–1,600	2/50	45–0	8 speeds	180	Yes	Yes	37
Rexon	SS13A	P	13/331	8	1,450	2/50	45–0	None	110	Yes	Yes	8.1/9
Rexon	SS16A	P	16/406	19	1,450	2/50	45–0	None	110	Yes	Yes	12/14

* The Hegner range has constant torque variable-speed options for these models

This is by no means an exhaustive list; it represents a selection of models currently available.

Conversion Table

Inches and their Equivalents in millimetres

Inch	0	1/16	1/8	3/16	1/4	5/16	3/8	7/16	1/2	9/16	5/8	11/16	3/4	13/16	7/8	15/16
0	0.0	1.6	3.2	4.8	6.4	7.9	9.5	11.1	12.7	14.3	15.9	17.5	19.1	20.6	22.2	23.8
1	25.4	27.0	28.6	30.2	31.7	33.3	34.9	36.5	38.1	39.7	41.3	42.9	44.4	46.0	47.6	49.2
2	50.8	52.4	54.0	55.6	57.1	58.7	60.3	61.9	63.5	65.1	66.7	68.3	69.8	71.4	73.0	74.6
3	76.2	77.8	79.4	81.0	82.5	84.1	85.7	87.3	88.9	90.5	92.1	93.7	95.2	96.8	98.4	100.0
4	101.6	103.2	104.8	106.4	108.0	109.5	111.1	112.7	114.3	115.9	117.5	119.1	120.7	122.2	123.8	125.4
5	127.0	128.6	130.2	131.8	133.4	134.9	136.5	138.1	139.7	141.3	142.9	144.5	146.1	147.6	149.2	150.8
6	152.4	154.0	155.6	157.2	158.8	160.3	161.9	163.5	164.1	166.7	168.3	169.9	171.5	173.0	174.6	176.2
7	177.8	179.4	181.0	182.6	184.2	185.7	187.3	188.9	190.5	192.1	193.7	195.3	196.9	198.4	200.0	201.6
8	203.2	204.8	206.4	208.0	209.6	211.1	212.7	214.3	215.9	217.5	219.1	220.7	222.3	223.8	225.4	227.0
9	228.6	230.2	231.8	233.4	235.0	236.5	238.1	239.7	241.3	242.9	244.5	246.1	247.7	249.2	250.8	252.4
10	254.0	255.6	257.2	258.8	260.4	261.9	263.5	265.1	266.7	268.3	269.9	271.5	273.1	274.6	276.2	277.8
11	279.4	281.0	282.6	284.2	285.7	287.3	288.9	290.5	292.1	293.7	295.3	296.9	298.4	300.0	301.6	303.2
12	304.8	306.4	308.0	309.6	311.1	312.7	314.3	315.9	317.5	319.1	320.7	322.3	323.8	325.4	327.0	328.6
13	330.2	331.8	333.4	335.0	336.5	338.1	339.7	341.3	342.9	344.5	346.1	347.7	349.2	350.8	352.4	354.0
14	355.6	357.2	358.8	360.4	361.9	363.5	365.1	366.7	368.3	369.9	371.5	373.1	374.6	376.2	377.8	379.4
15	381.0	382.6	384.2	385.8	387.3	388.9	390.5	392.1	393.7	395.3	396.9	398.5	400.0	401.6	403.2	404.8
16	406.4	408.0	409.6	411.2	412.7	414.3	415.9	417.5	419.1	420.7	422.3	423.9	425.4	427.0	428.6	430.2
17	431.8	433.4	435.0	436.6	438.1	439.7	441.3	442.9	444.5	446.1	447.7	449.3	450.8	452.4	454.0	455.6
18	457.2	458.8	460.4	462.0	463.5	465.1	466.7	468.3	469.9	471.5	473.1	474.7	476.2	477.8	479.4	481.0
19	482.6	484.2	485.8	487.4	488.9	490.5	492.1	493.7	495.3	496.9	498.5	500.1	501.6	503.2	504.8	506.4
20	508.0	509.6	511.2	512.8	514.3	515.9	517.5	519.1	520.7	522.3	523.9	525.5	527.0	528.6	530.2	531.8
21	533.4	535.0	536.6	538.2	539.7	541.3	542.9	544.5	546.1	547.7	549.3	550.9	552.4	554.0	555.6	557.2
22	558.8	560.4	562.0	563.6	565.1	566.7	568.3	569.9	571.5	573.1	574.7	576.3	577.8	579.4	581.0	582.6
23	584.2	585.8	587.4	589.0	590.5	592.1	593.7	595.3	596.9	598.5	600.1	601.7	603.2	604.8	606.4	608.0

Glossary

Ancillary 'table' A table made from thin material such as plywood, hardboard, Masonite or MDF, to cover all or part of the original saw-table. A hole is pierced in or near its centre, only big enough to permit the threading of the blade, thus giving support to the workpiece close to the cutting edge. Alternatively the blade may be used to cut a path in the ancillary table up to the point at which the sawyer determines it is to rest. It is then fixed by clamping or with blocks glued to its underside to facilitate fast re-location on the original table.

Boulle, Andre-Charles An 18th-century French marquetarian craftsman who developed styles and refined techniques that still survive. The École Boulle in Paris is a living testament to his work.

Bowsaw An early type of saw made from bending a naturally straight wooden or metal beam into an arc to the ends of which are attached the ends of a saw-blade. The tension in the blade is maintained by the spring in the arc attempting to return to its normal straight condition. Later refinements included tensioning devices, such as the application of a so-called Spanish windlass.

BSF B = Blade. S = Speed. F = Feed. A simple reference to considerations of the desirable balancing of the three ingredients of successful scroll-sawing. Easily remembered as Best Sawing Fundamentals.

C-frame Shaped like a letter 'c' whose open ends are usually equipped with small clamps used to grip the ends of a saw-blade. Being rigid, the frame has a pivot fitted upon which it swings vertically through an arc.

Coping saw A small hand saw of the c-frame variety whose blade may be rotated by releasing the tension maintained by the screw-action of its handle.

'Donkey' A machine favoured by French marquetarians during the 19th century, and constructed from wooden members incorporating a seat for the operator. Its parallel-arm was activated manually on a push-pull principle.

Dust blower Part of the standard equipment of good-quality machines, providing a constant flow of air from an independently motorized pump. Its nozzle outlet may be positioned to clear dust generated by the saw-blade.

Dust puffer A bellows-driven device providing a regular but intermittent supply of air for dust clearance from the sawing area. The action of the upper arm is used to depress and thus activate the bellows function.

Encrustation Literally, to overlay with a crust or hard coating, but the term is applied to many forms of inlaid work.

Extraction port An orifice located near the sawing area on a machine, such as under the table beneath the lower blade-clamp. It is intended to be coupled to a vacuum extraction device for positive dust removal.

Feed The term used to describe the rate at which the material is 'fed' towards the blade during the sawing operation.

Fence Fitted temporarily onto the saw-table at a pre-determined distance from the blade, this attachment serves as a guide against which the workpiece is placed and leant during traversing whilst the sawing action produces a theoretically parallel cut.

'Finger' fence Specially made to permit the sawing of a curved line to produce a parallel cut.

Fretsaw Name given to manual frame saws used for marquetry and other fine work. Motorized types are now more frequently referred to as scrollsaws, but either name is acceptable.

Golden Rule *See* BSF.

Guard Fitted to certain machines, usually attached to the upper frame, but sometimes on a separate extended bracket, the guard provides a partial barrier between the saw and the fingers of the operator.

Hold-down This is a misnomer, in that it prevents the workpiece from rising, rather than to hold it in some fixed position. It is frequently incorporated into the design of the guard.

Inlay A motif or object prepared for insertion into a prepared orifice. The term also describes the practice of so doing.

Intarsia Taken today to refer to a type of marquetry using pieces thick enough to permit light relief carving to give a three dimensional illusion.

Kerf The slot or gap left in the work-piece by the saw-blade. It is wider than the blade itself, since the width, or 'set' of the teeth is wider and allows clear passage of the blade.

'Leaving the line' When the marked line defining a portion to be sawn, remains as a border 'left', if so desired, on the portion for subsequent reference.

Luthier Once taken to mean a lute-maker, but now used to describe a maker of any type of musical instrument.

Marking knife A short-bladed knife used to scribe lines to indicate measurements, or for any other visual reference used in preference to a pencil line in cases where precision is required.

Marking-gauge This is a hand-sized device comprising a beam with a small blade used in marking a line parallel to a straight edge. To permit adjustment for length the beam is fitted into a hole, in a block that acts as the edge guide.

Marquetarian A person who practices the craft of marquetry. Marqueter is also used.

Marquetry The design, cutting and fitting together of pieces of wood veneer that are laid onto a ground, to depict patterns or pictorial effects. From the Old French *marque*, meaning to mark, as with a knife.

MDF Medium density fibreboard: a common, man-made, wood-based panel product. The word 'medium' suggests that other densities are available and this is so, but less commonly. Being of uniform thickness and lacking directional grain, the material lends itself to many uses.

NVR switch A no voltage release switch, is one that switches to the 'off' position if mains power is discontinued. This provides the safety feature of staying 'off' if power is supplied until manually placed in the 'on' position.

Parallel-arm Refers to a type of motorized scrollsaw where upper and lower arms are pivoted independently, but connected at the rear with a rod and at the front with the saw-blade, causing parallel motion when activated.

Pin-end blade One that has at each end, a cross-pin intended to be retained in a corresponding stirrup arrangement at the ends of the upper and lower arms of the scrollsaw frame. This type of blade is the ultimate in quick assembly since no clamps are necessary.

Pitch A short, alternative term referring to the amount of teeth in a given measurement, as for example, 6t.p.i, meaning 6 teeth per inch.

Plain-ended blade A term to differentiate this type of blade from the pin-ended variety, being itself without cross-pins, thus plain-ended.

'Sandwich' Sometimes called 'stack' or 'pack' cutting where two or more veneers are fixed together in a layer and sawn simultaneously.

Sawyers Generic term applied to those practitioners of sawing, of any kind, manual or mechanized.

'Skip-tooth' A blade that has one or more teeth removed from its otherwise regular row that normally would have no gaps, other than those provided by the backing down of the points to the troughs between the teeth.

'Splitting' the line If a blade is narrow enough by comparison with the width of the marked line, it is possible to leave an equal amount of the mark on either side. This provides a visual reference to each part of the then divided workpiece.

s.p.m. Where s = strokes, p = per and m = minute. Generally meant to indicate the speed of the reciprocating saw frame.

Spring-return A type of scrollsaw that has a fixed upper arm, to which is attached one end of the saw-blade. Incorporated in the clamping device is a tension spring that draws back the blade to its original, higher, position after the downward stroke has been made by the downward movement of the moving lower arm. The lower clamp is fixed without a spring.

t.p.i Teeth per inch, *see* pitch.

U.G.No Universal Generic Number: an attempt to create a standard means of specifying the design of blades in terms of size and type. A laudable system as yet unadopted by all manufacturers.

Index